The Jones Guide

to

Fitness & Health

in New York

❁

1999

Chris,

for your

nycity trips.

Se

The Jones Guide
to
Fitness & Health
in New York

❁

Kathy Myers Jones

With an Introduction
by Terry Trucco

CITY & COMPANY
NEW YORK

Publisher's Note

Neither City & Company nor the author has any interest, financial or personal, in the locations listed in this book. No fees were paid or services rendered in exchange for inclusion in these pages.

Please note that every effort was made to ensure that information regarding phone numbers, hours and fees was accurate and up-to-date at the time of publication, but these are subject to change. All class and session times are one hour unless otherwise noted in text.

City & Company
22 West 23rd Street
New York, NY 10010

Printed in the United States of America

Cover Illustration by Katherine Mahoney
Design by Rebecca Aidlin

Library of Congress Cataloging-in-publication Data is available upon request.
ISBN 1-885492-13-8

First Edition

Acknowledgments

In pursuit of fitness...special thanks to Lynn for inspiration, Rekha for much needed assistance, Susan for editorial counsel, Glenn for computer expertise, and Cary for emotional support. And to all who trained, educated and guided me on my journey towards health and fitness.

Contents

Introduction ◆ xv
In the Beginning ◆ xix

Studio Classes

Members Only

GYMS

HEALTH CLUBS AND FITNESS CENTERS

◆ IX

Equinox Fitness Club ◆ 25
Excelsior Athletic Club ◆ 26
Executive Fitness Center at The New York Vista Hotel ◆ 27
Gold's Gym ◆ 28
Manhattan Plaza Health Club ◆ 29
New York Health & Racquet Club ◆ 30
Peninsula Spa ◆ 31
Printing House Fitness and Racquet Club ◆ 32
Profile Health Spa ◆ 33
Reebok Sports Club New York ◆ 34
Sheraton Manhattan Fitness Center ◆ 35
Sheraton New York Health Club ◆ 36
Soho Training Center ◆ 37
United Nations Park Hyatt Health Club ◆ 38
Vertical Club ◆ 39
World Gym ◆ 40

THE Ys

92nd Street Y Center for Health, Fitness & Sport ◆ 42
West Side YMCA ◆ 43
Neighborhood Y Locations ◆ 45

One-on-One Training

Yoga & Meditation

Martial Arts

T'AI CHI

KARATE

AIKIDO

Movement & Bodywork

ALEXANDER TECHNIQUE

PILATES

Neighborhood Index ◆ 95
Subject Index ◆ 101

✱ Introduction

I became an exercise convert twelve years ago when my husband came home from a five-mile run, flushed, sweaty and happily swigging Gatorade. Was he tired? Pleasantly. But after spending a sunny afternoon watching an old movie, I felt distinctly cranky, even a little jealous. His afternoon had been healthier and, oddly enough, more relaxing than mine. It was time to get moving.

The next day, in an old ballet leotard and tired sneakers, I shuffled into the back row of an aerobics class and tried to look as though I knew what I was doing. The instructor, a muscular Macho Man, wore a ridiculous tomato-red jumpsuit, but the steps sang, the stretches sizzled, the music pulsed, and the hour went by. Back home, flushed and sweaty, I broke out a Gatorade, and realized that I couldn't wait to go back.

I've been exercising ever since, two or three times a week, indulging in everything from two-hour aerobics classes to mind-soothing yoga, from vigorous power step sessions to anything that's new. If I can't take a class, I play on the weight machines, not nearly as fun as jumping around to loud music, but gratifying at meal time. Exercise that builds muscles allows you to consume more calories, the researchers tell us.

Exercise of any kind offers benefits. The immediate

payoffs of an exercise session are to reduce stress and lower your blood pressure. A long-term regimen of working out three times a week for 30 minutes dramatically reduces the risk of dying from heart disease, diabetes or stroke. Exercise is believed to promote mental health, beef up immunity and cut the risk of developing diseases like osteoporosis and certain cancers.

Exercise is also forgiving; you can start at any age and reap rich rewards. Research shows that strength-training can increase bone density in older people.

The trick is to exercise regularly and frequently. A daily blow-out isn't necessary; moderate moves, like a brisk walk on a treadmill, are beneficial, provided you partake regularly. In a recent pro-exercise declaration, the American College of Sports Medicine stated that every adult should get 30 minutes or more of moderate-intensity physical activity every day of the week, if possible.

Exercising in New York, like anything else in the city, is something of an art. It requires effort, expense and patience. Expect to book hours in advance for hot classes and to queue for the StairMaster at the smaller gyms. Expect to pay a lordly sum to join a health club that is half the size of a cheaper workout emporium in the suburbs.

But as this book shows, almost nowhere else are the choices so varied, the instructors so professional, the classes so cutting-edge and the participants so enthusiastic. Health clubs range from world-class spas, like the perfumey Peninsula, to the classic YMCAs, with generations of old sweat in the air. There's superb instruction in yoga, boxing and the martial arts. And signing up with a personal trainer who has also made a best-selling work-out video is a snap.

What's important is to find something you like, a regi-men you'll look forward to day after day, week after week. Chances are good that on the following pages you will find precisely that.

Terry Trucco
New York

❋ In the Beginning

In 1992, I spent more dollars than I care to remember trying to cure chronic sciatica aggravated by a bulging disc. The culprit was my favorite workout routine and the suggested solution was to stop exercising or get a personal trainer and re-evaluate my approach to fitness. I chose the latter. The courtship with the personal trainer was a costly one, and the sciatica was proving to be a formidable foe. The quest for ways to master my own body dynamics began. I tried everything, and in the process I began to think of you also. Perhaps you were in the same predicament as me, or would simply like to exercise your fitness options and try a new program.

Over time, this guide has grown to encompass a wide range of health and fitness programs currently being offered around the city for nurturing body, mind and spirit. It tries to meet the needs of fitness buffs, novices, children, senior citizens, those recovering from injury, as well as the pregnant, the physically challenged and those suffering from heart problems, arthritis or diabetes. The entries include what I consider to be the leaders in each category of fitness. Their dedication to providing quality instruction, information, equipment and service is unsurpassed. And my apologies to those of value who have been omitted, inadvertently or for lack of space.

XX ◆ IN THE BEGINNING

There are over 100 choices here, divided into six sections: studio classes, membership programs, one-on-one training, yoga and meditation, martial arts and movement studies. Within these sections are listed dozens of programs, classes, services and facilities existing in the city: water exercise, aerobic classes, boxing, weight-training, tennis, racquetball, squash, basketball, massage, wellness, nutritional guidance, exercise for pregnant moms, even baby-sitting. Turn to one of the indexes in the back of the book for a quick take on what's in your neighborhood or look up a particular area of interest.

For those looking to begin a fitness routine, I suggest sampling a few programs to get grounded in the basics, i.e., to build a strong center and torso, address postural alignment and learn stretching techniques. A beginner yoga class or back care exercise regime would address these concepts. For something more advanced, try a Pilates Mat class, which is a cost effective way to learn the exercises and benefit from the methodology.

To address specific body-building needs, consult the roster of one-on-one services or movement practitioners. Or sample a few gyms where body-building is de-rigueur and trainers can be recommended. For a gentle approach to relieve tension-holding patterns caused by repetitive motion injury or misuse, I suggest exploring the hands-on approach of the Alexander Technique. For a careful review of a fitness regime that has gone awry, try a one-on-one session with a physical therapist or movement analyst.

To your health and your journey. Experiment, enjoy

and share with us your discoveries, new haunts and suggestions. We would love to include them in our next edition.

Kathy Myers Jones

✿ Studio Classes

One of the great pleasures of the exercise world is shopping—visiting different studios and sampling single classes just for fun. A variety of studios in New York City provide single classes in everything from the predictable (body sculpting, toning, aerobics) to the less so.

At Circus Gym, for example, offerings include classes on the trapeze and tight wire. And Doug Stern's deep water running class, which avoids the stress of pavement pounding, is taught in a pool, where students strap on flotation belts.

Single classes are like garnishes, perfect for spicing up a fitness routine that has become a bit flat. And for those in the market for a regimen, they are a smart, inexpensive way to compare teachers, size up studios and try out classes. There's no rule, after all, that says single classes can't become multiples.

BACK IN SHAPE
37 West 54th Street ◆ 245-9131
Hours: Open daily, class times vary.

Getting back into shape becomes a social occasion in the girls' club ambiance of Marjorie Jaffee's studio where the exchange of banter between exercises is the norm. Individual assessments and small classes produce the personalized attention that has attracted a loyal following among older women. Jaffee's philosophy, "muscles make bones move," stems from her training with Dr. Sonya Weber, the founder of Columbia Presbyterian Posture and Back Care Clinic. Her classes focus on teaching proper body alignment and supportive muscle conditioning. **FEES:** One class $16. Call for schedule.

CALLANETICS STUDIO OF MANHATTAN
154 West 57th Street ◆ 765-2900
Hours: Mon - Fri: 7 am - 7:30 pm; Sat: 8:30 am - 6 pm; Sun: 9 am - 12:30 pm.

As soon as franchises became available to teach The Method Callan in 1991, Ruth Jeffries took the training program, obtained the required certification and currently operates the only Callanetics studio in Manhattan. Her split-level studio loft in distinguished Carnegie Hall provides an intimate setting for small classes of six to eight in which she individually trains clients to shape their muscles with tiny, focused, gentle movements. The method ensures a safe, effective workout, especially for those recovering from injury. Video sales and rentals are also available. **FEES:** One class $25; 10 classes $180.

CIRCUS GYM
2121 Broadway ◆ 799-3755
Hours: Open Mon - Sat, class times vary.

Former competitive gymnasts Allison and Nora Cooper transported their enthusiasm for the circus arts into a complete gymnasium, replete with circus accouterments. Students are taught circus skills on tight wire, single trapeze, Spanish web and rings, all in preparation for a performance given at the conclusion of the training program. Gymnastic equipment includes an 18-foot tumble track, high balance beam and air trampoline. The teachers are circus performers, gymnasts and dancers. Safety is key here and strict adherence is paid to the guidelines for instruction established by the U.S. Gymnastic Foundation. **SERVICES & FEES:** Private classes for adults can be arranged; Mommy & Me for ages 6 mos. to 2 yrs.; children 3 to 6 years cover skill levels 1 - 5; children 7 to 15 years cover levels 5 - 10; 19 week program (once a week) $389; multiple weekly classes are discounted.

DOUG STERN'S DEEP WATER RUNNING
222-0720
John Jay College (Mon)
889 Tenth Avenue
Columbia Grammar and Preparatory School (Wed & Thurs)
5 West 93rd Street
Hours: Mon: 7 and 7:50 pm; Wed - Thurs: 6:10 and
6:55 pm.

When Doug Stern isn't running competitively, he's teaching deep water running. For marathoners in training, running in water provides ideal low-impact cross training. Runners wear a flotation belt and are encouraged to maintain good form during three-minute circuits, alternating downhill and uphill strides. After 45 minutes of this, you float home. **FEES:** One class $15; seven classes $75.

GLEASON'S GYM
75 Front Street, Brooklyn ◆ 718-797-2872
Hours: Mon - Fri: 7 am - 8 pm; Sat: 8:30 am - 4 pm.

This is authentic training in the art of boxing at the only pro gym in the city. It's been around since 1937, and the only thing that has changed is the location. The staff has turned out 109 world champions, including Mohammed Ali and Roberto Durand. All the professionals train here, as well as actors, models and business executives. They trained Robert De Niro for his role in *Raging Bull*, and they'll train you, too. One of sixty-two trainers will have you jump rope, don mitts, and practice rounds on the heavy bag and speed bag; when you're ready, they'll arrange sparring matches in one of four padded, regulation-size rings. The buzzer rings every three minutes, designating a minute of down time. You'll even begin to look like a fighter with long, lean muscles and the stamina of a distance runner. **FEES:** One and a half hour session with a trainer $10; monthly $45. Gleason's is currently seeking a Manhattan location.

JEFF MARTIN AEROBIC EXERCISE STUDIO
403 East 91st Street ◆ 996-2626
Hours: Open daily, class times vary.

Jeff Martin, the Jam Master, considers himself a talent agent. Thirteen years ago, he paved the way for the birth of jazz aerobics. Today, the instructors he selects and trains—actresses, waiters and dancers—are known for their signature classes providing exciting, innovative choreography. In her class called Cardio Moves, Patricia Moreno spews out endless combinations of skillfully executed steps for her enamored followers to duplicate; the more crowded it is, the more people want to take it. MTV choreographer Devora Cooper teaches Hip-Hop; Annie Niland, national step trainer for Reebok, leads a wildly popular step class. There are no slouch teachers here. Classes in power yoga, shadow boxing and body sculpting are also available. **SERVICES & FEES:** Baby-sitting available Mon - Fri: 10 am - 12 pm; one class $12; 10 classes $99.

LOTTE BERK METHOD, LTD.
23 East 67th Street ◆ 288-6613
Hours: Mon - Fri: 7:30 am - 7 pm; Sat - Sun: 8:30 am - 2:30 pm.

For 23 years instructors of the Lotte Berk Method have taught, nurtured and reshaped the bodies of the affluent and educated. With students engaged in the "Lotte Berk" tuck—pelvis tipped forward, glutes tight, abs in—the focus is on maintaining correct body alignment through a series of movements that incorporate principles of ballet, yoga and orthopedic exercises. This is often the choice of people recovering from injury, excessive training or incorrect exercise habits. It's a tough workout, so don't feel glum about being placed in the beginner's class—you'll be grateful later. **FEES:** One class $16; 20 classes $298.

LUYE AQUAFIT
310 East 23rd Street ◆ 505-2400
Classes taught at Talent Unlimited High School Pool, 317 East 68th Street
Hours: Mon, Wed and Thurs: 6, 7 and 8 pm; Tues: 6 and 7 pm; Sat: 9, 10 and 11 am. Children 5 to 12 years, Sat: 12 pm.

Everybody into the pool! Luye packs a wallop of a workout, integrating cardio fitness with weight-training and body sculpting, all in an hour—and you never leave the pool. She keeps the pace moving as you tone upper and lower body with the assistance of leg buoys and hand paddles. Master Russian dance steps and jog to the beat of Billy Joel. It's fun, it's fit and it's safer in the water. An all-around feel-good workout especially attractive to those recovering from injuries and to cross-trainers. **FACILITIES:** The locker rooms are a labyrinth of shower stalls; hair dryers are provided but bring your own soap, shampoo and towel. **FEES:** 10-week aquatic program (one class weekly) $190.

MANHATTAN BODY
149 East 72nd Street ◆ 772-6087
Hours: Mon - Fri: 6:45 am - 7:15 pm; Sat: 9 am - 5:15 pm; Sun: 9 am - 12 pm.

Sole proprietor Ann Picirillo likes to keep her non-power-house studio simple. "Stay fit and avoid injury" is her motto. Classes in body toning and non-impact step are offered on an alternating schedule daily. The latest resistance gadgets, power rings and thigh-master are used for toning and sculpting and for coaxing lazy muscles to work harder. Ten staff instructors and varied programming keep classes interesting and participants motivated. **SERVICES & FEES:** Swedish and Shiatsu massage, reflexology, sports injury therapy and aromatherapy by appointment $60; one class $15; 10 classes $140.

MOVEMENTS AFOOT

31 West 21st Street ◆ 675-9614

Bringing together the best information available on body awareness and conditioning, owner Lesley Powell has pooled some of the top talent in the city. Here's a sampling of class programs: Body/Mind Yoga with Doris Pasteleur teaches the fundamentals for moving into yoga postures, getting grounded, recognizing disharmony in weight distribution and maintaining effortless breathing. Connective Tissue Therapy with John Chanik focuses on hands-on body work to stimulate the interconnective tissues of the body and break down adhesions in the fascia. Bartenieff Fundamentals and Fundamentally Fit teaches participants movement initiation and sequencing, weight shift and spatial relation, breath and core body support. The Breath & Movement class with Marion von Haslingen is based on the work of Ilse Middendorf and teaches students how to increase sensory awareness of the breath—"the innermost core of our being." Release into Strength with Lisa Trank integrates principles of the Alexander technique with a series of movements designed to develop body awareness. The Physio Ball Workout emphasizes balance and alignment by instructing students to center their weight on large physio balls while performing stretching and toning exercises. **SERVICES & FEES:** All classes $12; private training and massage available by appointment.

NEW YORK SPACES
131 West 72nd Street ♦ 799-5433
939 Eighth Avenue ♦ 799-5433
Hours: Mon - Fri: 10 am - 11 pm; Sat - Sun: 10 am - 9 pm.

This is where Madonna rehearses and Lauren Bacall works on her pre-production routines. More than 40 independent teachers book space here for classes ranging from body sculpting, stretch, yoga, and aerobics to jujitsu, ballet, mambo, tango and ballroom dancing. When Patricia Ripley isn't busy overseeing, she's teaching her brand of low-impact step for beginners and intermediates. **FEES:** One class $8 - $12. Union discounts available. Studio space available by the hour/day/week.

PEGGY LEVINE STUDIO
212 West 92nd Street ♦ 749-1378
Hours: Mon - Fri: 9:15 am - 7:15 pm; Sat: 9:15 am - 1:15 pm; Sun: 9:30 am - 12:15 pm.

Pre-natal, post-natal, body sculpting and child care—Levine's got it all well covered. Staying within the guidelines established by the American College of Obstetrics and Gynecology, her classes provide a safe, effective way to exercise through pregnancy and to establish endurance for birthing. Peggy trained with the Elizabeth Bing Center for Parenting and is certified to teach the Lamaze Method. **SERVICES & FEES:** Baby-sitting $1 per child; one class $14; eight classes $101.

RADU'S PHYSICAL CULTURE STUDIO
24 West 57th Street ◆ 759-9617
Hours: Mon - Fri: 7 am - 7 pm; Sat: 10 am - 1 pm;
Sun: 11 am - 5 pm.

Remember grade school gym class? Squat thrusts, jump-ing jacks, push-ups, running relay races around the gym? Welcome back. The legendary Radu's compulsory curriculum reflects his concept of physical culture—com-bining sports-training techniques with cardiovascular conditioning to improve one's physical abilities to master sports. Once you get the techniques down, it's on to the court for a round of basketball or a game of volleyball. Or, you can duke it out with Radu in the ring. P.S. There are no mirrors in the new studio for you to witness the process or exult in the results. **SERVICES & FEES:** One-on-one with Radu $100; with staff $65; one class $16; 10 classes $140.

▦ Members Only

In a city with some of the costliest real estate on earth, health clubs and gyms, with their generous proportions, seem the ultimate luxury. Fortunately, New York City has a facility for nearly every need and pocketbook, from sybaritic spas with eucalyptus steam rooms and StairMasters overlooking the rivers to crowded gyms with a zillion members and a feeling of intensity in the air. For swimming enthusiasts, gyms and health clubs often provide the only way to indulge regularly in the city.

Gyms tend to be straight-up, minimum-frill places that focus on weight-training, body building and cardiovascular conditioning. Health clubs, in contrast, use frills to reel in members, even at the more spartan outposts. Besides classes, the requisite machines and occasionally a pool, expect to find cafes, baby-sitters, locker rooms and spa services from reflexology to massage. And in a class by themselves are the Ys. Though old, big and often a bit brute, they consistently serve up top-notch machinery, basketball courts, volleyball and some of the biggest, and best, pools in town. And you can't beat the price.

 Gyms

CHELSEA GYM

262 West 17th Street ◆ 255-1150
Hours: Mon - Fri: 6 am - 12 am; Sat - Sun: 9 am - 12 am.

When Louis Nelson acquired this classic brownstone in 1983, he turned it into a mecca for bodybuilders. Spread out over three floors, this all-male-revue gym offers an extensive array of free weights and Cybex equipment. Six full-time trainers are on hand to assist in weight-training programs, aerobic circuit training and abdominal exercises. **FITNESS EQUIPMENT:** StairMasters, LifeCycle and LifeRower. **FACILITIES:** Steam, sauna, tanning beds and a roof-top sun deck replete with faux grass and lounging chairs. **SERVICES & FEES:** One-on-one training session $55; Shiatsu, Swedish and sports massage by appointment $55; guests $65; annual membership $499; one visit $12.

DAVID BARTON GYM

552 Avenue of the Americas ◆ 727-0004
30 East 85th Street ◆ 517-7577
Hours: Mon - Fri: 6 am - 12 am; Sat: 9 am - 9 pm;
Sun: 10 am - 11 pm.

Why do people work out? To "look better naked," says Barton. In his downtown office, the former Mr. Northeast body-building champ scopes the workout floor—10,000 square feet filled with custom built and top-of-the-line equipment. It's after 5:00 pm, and the place is beginning to fill up. The abs class offered every 60 minutes just started. On-floor spotters are offering pointers to clients who are lifting weights. Barton personally trains his 15 trainers and retrains them regularly. In the adjoining cardio-fitness room, clients on steppers, bikes and treadmills are watching an old Fellini film on a giant screen. The fashion-and-media crowd gathered here expects nothing less. **FITNESS EQUIPMENT:** Criterion, Cybex, Polaris, Icarian, Hammer Strength and Heartline, a full range of free weights, Quinton and LifeFitness treadmills, StairMasters and LifeCycles. **SERVICES & FEES:** One-on-one training session $60; 20 sessions $800; one-year membership $659 with $149 initiation fee and $59 monthly includes one free training session; day pass $15; club reciprocity with Miami facility.

PRESCRIPTIVES FITNESS GYM
250 West 54th Street ◆ 307-7760
Hours: Mon - Fri: 6 am - 12 pm; Sat: 8 am - 10 pm;
Sun: 9 am - 10 pm.

There is a doctor in the house—and a comedian too! One flight-up, Dr. Gary Prince treats sports injuries and prescribes rehabilitation programs. Pro-trainer Valerie Green runs the show downstairs. She'll personally oversee your workout or team you up with one of 15 in-house trainers. **FITNESS EQUIPMENT:** More than 70 pieces of top-of-the-line cardio equipment including CardioSquats, CrossAerobic Kayak and StepMills, NordicTracks, PT4000 StairMasters, ClimbMax, BikeMax, LifeCycle recumbent bikes, VersaClimber, Upper-Body Ergometer, and Super Trotters cover the gamut of possibilities for cross-training, rehabilitation and general workout programs. Weight-training includes free weights, full circuit of Icarian, plus select pieces of Cybex, Body Masters and Tk Star. And if it's laughter you're after, stick around. Co-owner Dana Carvey and his fellow cohorts from *Saturday Night Live* have been known to practice their antics while pumping-up. **SERVICES & FEES:** One-on-one training session $45; 14 month membership $375; day pass $12.

PUMPING IRON GYMS
403 East 91st Street ♦ 996-5444
2162 Broadway ♦ 496-2444
Hours: Mon - Fri: 6 am - 12 pm; Sat - Sun: 8 am - 9 pm.

The overnight success of the 1983 movie *Pumping Iron* catapulted body building into the fitness mainstream. Broadway bodybuilders and partners Frank Ferrante and James Meceda, adopted the name and evolved into the deities of body building. Most members here bring their own trainers. Frank can help with recommendations or team you up with one of the five in-house trainers who'll put a program together for you, then check on you regularly. The 6,000 square-foot gym is carefully designed with sequential work stations and free-weight areas. No TV screens, no music-induced clamor and no Doc Martens, please: Sneakers only. **FITNESS EQUIPMENT:** Weight-resistance, Tk Star, David and Cybex, plus a full range of free weights. Cardio includes Trotters, NordicTrack, VersaClimber and LifeCycles. **SERVICES & FEES:** Training session $45 - $70; day pass $10; three months $175; annual membership $600.

▨ Health Clubs and Fitness Centers

AMERICAN FITNESS CENTER
128 Eighth Avenue ◆ 627-0065
Hours: Mon - Fri: 6 am - 12 am; Sat - Sun: 9 am - 9 pm.

This new full-service coed club (with a bent towards men) addresses fitness and wellness. Madison Park Physical Therapy recently opened shop on the premises with a full staff and six treatment rooms, including one for traction. The wrap-around cafe downstairs overlooks the cardio and circuit-training area, where there are 20,000 square feet of equipment to muscle with. Twenty one-on-one trainers are on staff; their special peak-performance training program is receiving kudos from sports enthusiasts. Check out the splash art montage on the downstairs wall, compliments of local Soho artist Jack Gooch. **FITNESS EQUIPMENT:** Three complete Cybex circuits and work-out stations feature Hammer Strength, Nautilus free weights, StairMasters, LifeCycles, Concept II rowers, VersaClimbers and more. TVs are strategically suspended at all angles and individually stationed on cardio equipment; bring a headset. **CLASSES:** "Abs, Buns, Thighs," step, boxing (speed bag and heavy bag) and yoga. **FACILITIES:** Free sauna, steam, tanning beds, all amenities and towel service. **SERVICES & FEES:** One-on-one training session $60; ten sessions $500; Swedish, sports, deep tissue, Shiatsu and acupressure massage $50; membership (peak hours) $699; off-peak $499; guest fee $15.

APEX
205 East 85th Street ◆ 737-8377
Hours: Mon - Fri: 6 am - 9 pm; Sat - Sun: 8 am - 6 pm.

Everything here is perfect. Liz Oliver provides programming suitable for everyone in an environment both aesthetically pleasing and ecologically sound. The glassed-in studios are light and airy. Black-and-white photographs of athletes from the twenties inspire and amuse. With an ambitious staff, more than 92 classes a week to choose from and a roster of celebrity teachers that reads like a who's who among the fitness elite, the place starts hopping at 6:00 am. Seniors arrive for mid-morning classes and schoolchildren dominate the studios in late afternoon. By 5:00 pm, the high-energy crowd takes over. Fourteen personal trainers certified by the American College of Sports Medicine provide fitness evaluations, one-on-one training and high-tech nutritional guidance. You can take a break at the cafe where the juice is fresh-squeezed, the food nutritious, fresh and fat-free. **FITNESS EQUIPMENT:** Full Cybex circuit, Precor treadmills, Alpine and LifeSteps, Bodyguard StairMaster, NordicTrack, Concept II rower, Upper-Body Ergometer, recumbent bike and a full range of free weights. **CLASSES:** Aerobic, step, walk Reebok, interval training, knock-out workout, body sculpting, stretch, Alexander Technique, Pilates Mat, Seido karate for adults and children and Senior Swing. **SERVICES & FEES:** Fitness evaluation $85; one-on-one-training session $65; one class $17; 20-class card (two-month expiration) $225. Membership is available on request.

ASPHALT GREEN
1750 York Avenue ◆ 369-8890
Pool Hours: Mon - Fri: 5:30 am - 3 pm;
Sat - Sun: 8 am - 8 pm.
Fitness Center Hours: Mon - Fri: 5:30 am - 10 pm.

Once the site of New York City's municipal asphalt manufacturing plant, this 5.5-acre location has been transformed into a state-of-the-art, 74,000 square-foot aquatics, sports and fitness complex. With a mission to serve the community and promote a lifetime of wellness, the center offers a broad range of services, classes and membership programs. The aqua center, the focus of activity, features an Olympic-standard 50-meter indoor pool with special features designed to accommodate adults, children and the disabled. **FITNESS EQUIPMENT:** State-of-the-art Cybex, LifeCycle, StairMaster, Gravitron, NordicTrack, LifeSteps, Life Stride treadmills, Biodex, free weights and more. **CLASSES:** Aerobics, step, body sculpting, yoga, stretch, water exercises, healthy heart, breath & relaxation, fitness basics, low impact and yoga. Classes for people with disabilities include yoga, seated aerobics, wheelchair basketball, and water programs. Organized youth programs include indoor and outdoor soccer, karate, gymnastics, basketball, football and tennis. **FACILITIES:** Indoor and outdoor tracks, volleyball and basketball courts. Locker rooms are equipped with steam and sauna. **SERVICES & FEES:** One-on-one training session (members) $50; non-members $60. Swedish and sports massage (members) $50; non-members $60; basic annual adult membership $1,188; senior discounts available; guest fee fitness or swim $14; swim and fitness $25; class cards available for non-members.

BETTER BODIES
22 West 19th Street ◆ 929-6789
Hours: Mon - Fri: 6:30 am - 10:30 pm;
Sat - Sun: 8 am - 8 pm.

This is body building with a twist. The cafe provides a soothing entrance to the tremendous amount of steel you will encounter in this 20,000 plus square-foot gym. Brian Moss's cavernous underground sub-culture, an oasis for the body-building elite, boasts one of the most extensive ranges of weight-lifting equipment in town. Frequently scouted for its atmosphere by local photographers, the club has color-speckled walls and second-hand couches that juxtapose well with the utilitarian equipment. The newly created cross-training center, featuring classes in boxer aerobics and athletic training, pleases the growing 2,000 plus membership. **FITNESS EQUIPMENT:** Hammer Strength (14 pieces), Icarian, BodyMaster, full range of free weights, a specially designed squat rack and chin-up bar, Cybex, semi-recumbent and upright bikes, Tectrix StairMasters, StairMaster Cross Robic, and StarTrac. **CLASSES:** Boxing training with Mark Breland, Massive Cardio and martial-arts training with Michael Schwartz, Pump (weight-training) with Brian Moss, athletic training classes, plus a full range of step and aerobic classes. **SERVICES & FEES:** One-on-one training session $50; unlimited classes plus cardiovascular and weight-training $599; unlimited classes plus cardiovascular $499; single weight room visit $8; class card $10.

BODY ELITE

131 East 31st Street ◆ 213-1408
Hours: Mon - Thurs: 6 am - 12 pm; Fri: 6 am - 10 pm;
Sat - Sun: 9 am - 7 pm.

Nine years ago, when Russell Henis stopped strutting at Chippendales, the Cornell grad redirected his business expertise towards selling health. Not trying to make this a status gym, Henis aims to appeal to those seeking to maintain a moderate level of fitness in a non-competitive atmosphere. On hand to provide encouragement is a qualified staff of one-on-one trainers. The myriad cardio and weight-training equipment jockeying for space makes the most out of tight quarters in this street-level, 12,000 square foot-gym. Nautilus and free weights, plus an exercise studio, are stationed downstairs. Corporate executives and local residents keep the place hopping and a bevy of dancers granted carte blanche by management are known to frequent the tanning beds. **FITNESS**

EQUIPMENT: Full Cybex circuit, Hammer Strength, free weights, Quinton and StarTrac treadmills, Tectrix bikes and StairMasters, PT 4000 StairMasters, Concept II rowers and VersaClimber. **CLASSES:** Full range of aerobic, step, body sculpting, box aerobics, yoga and ballroom dancing. **SERVICES & FEES:** One-on-one training $40 - $50; Swedish and Shiatsu massage $50; mini chair massage $1/minute; annual membership $699; off-peak $499; staff nutritionist and counseling included with membership orientation; day pass $15.

BODYSTRENGTH
250 West 106th Street ◆ 316-3338
Hours: Mon - Fri: 6:30 am - 10 pm;
Sat - Sun: 7:30 am - 7:30 pm.

Former dance team choreographers and graduates of Barbara Brennan's Healing Science Training, Bruce and Andes Bell bring a wide range of expertise to their well-established fitness programs. Their studio has been long recognized by Columbia University students and local residents as a top-notch source of innovative programming and quality instruction. Classes aim to teach awareness in movement and basic fitness concepts. Weight-training is available in the studio downstairs. Fitness classes and weight-training membership can be purchased separately. **FITNESS EQUIPMENT:** Full-circuit Cybex weight-resistance and free weights, Trotter treadmill, NextStep 1000 StairMaster, LifeCycle, VersaClimber. **CLASSES:** Full range of aerobic classes (low impact, funk and reggae-inspired), step, body sculpting, yoga and ballet. **SERVICES & FEES:** One-on-one training, evaluation and orientation $65 - $75; subsequent sessions $45 - $50; annual membership with unlimited classes plus cardio-vascular and weight-training equipment $816; weight room only $582; one class $12.50; 10 classes $99; passport program (two weeks of unlimited workouts for first-time clients only) $25/usage.

CARDIO FITNESS CENTERS
9 West 57th Street ◆ 753-3980
200 Park Avenue ◆ 682-4440
885 Third Avenue ◆ 888-2120
79 Maiden Lane ◆ 943-1510
Hours: Mon - Fri: 6:30 am - 9:30 pm; all clubs closed Sat - Sun except Park Avenue, open Sat - Sun: 9 am - 5 pm.

Established in 1977, Cardio Fitness has enjoyed a solid reputation among corporate executives for its clinical-medical approach to fitness. Now capitalizing on prestige and several spacious facilities, new programs address sports training, nutritional guidance and managed weight loss along with expanded testing services. **FITNESS EQUIPMENT:** Top-of-the-line Cybex, NordicTrack, LifeFitness, Unison, Keiser and free weights. Each cardio unit is equipped with a pulse-monitoring device. Twenty exercise physiologists and qualified trainers on staff provide individualized programs and nutritional guid-ance. **FACILITIES:** All locker room amenities plus sauna. **SERVICES & FEES:** Exercise clothing provided and laundered; one-on-one training session $45; annual membership $1,700; initiation fee $250; member guest $20; International Health and Racquet Sports Association club reciprocity; corporate membership programs available.

CLUB LA RAQUETTE
119 West 56th Street ◆ 245-1144
Hours: Mon - Fri: 6 am - 11 pm; Sat - Sun: 7 am - 8 pm.

The club's motto—providing total fitness—is reflected in the recent renovations. In the new 'cardio theater' area upstairs TVs are strung along the walls, providing listening and viewing options. There is ample top-of-the-line equipment comfortably divided among three workout stations plus a separate free weight room. A full range of classes is offered in two studios downstairs. Towering above the skyline and offering idyllic park views, the penthouse-level solarium pool is a quiet oasis for giving weary bodies over to soothing waters. **FITNESS EQUIPMENT:** Nautilus circuit (14 pieces), two full Cybex circuits, LifeCycles, two NordicTracks, StairMasters, Gravitron, LifeRowers, Smith, Paramount weight-resistance equipment and free weights. **FACILITIES:** 20 x 40-foot pool, half-size basketball court, roof-top track (1/24 mile), squash court and three racquetball courts. Whirlpool, sauna, spacious locker room with full amenities. **CLASSES:** Full range of aerobic, step, circuit, body sculpting, boxing, aqua aerobics, and yoga. **SERVICES & FEES:** Laundry and dry-cleaning; one-on-one training session $45; Swedish, deep tissue, Shiatsu, acupressure, sport massage by appointment $45 (also available to non-members); fitness plus pool membership $1,100; fitness only membership $800; International Health and Racquet Sports Association reciprocity.

CRUNCH FITNESS
54 East 13th Street ◆ 475-2018
162 West 83rd Street ◆ 875-1902
404 Lafayette Street ◆ 614-0120
Hours: Mon - Thurs: 7 am - 10 pm; Fri: 7 am - 8 pm;
Sat: 8:30 am - 7 pm; Sun: 10 am - 8 pm.

When Doug Levine's acting career faltered, he turned to his second great passion—aerobic fitness. In 1988 he opened Crunch Fitness to an enthusiastic Village crowd, and so began the Crunch phenomenon—Doug's aerobic blend of funk, hip-hop, slammin jam (street dances) done to Latin music, soft rap and big-band sounds. Inspired by street wear, he designed a full line of athletic apparel bearing the Crunch logo. Not bad for an out-of-work actor. Their recent renovations at the Thirteenth Street location boast new weight-training facilities and equipment, plus additional fitness studios. **FITNESS EQUIPMENT:** Weight-resistance includes complete circuit of Icarian plus full range of free weights. Cardio includes LifeCycles, Tectrix climbers, Gauntlet, VersaClimber and a separate boxing area featuring heavy bags and speed bags. **CLASSES:** New Step City, Diva Step, Spinning, Knockout Boxing, Hi/Lo-impact aerobics, PM Jam, Sweat Like Hell, Washboard Abs, yoga (Jivamukti,

Iyengar, traditional Hatha and Yogasol), belly dancing, body sculpt, stretch and more. At the Lafayette location a live D.J. provides music for the aerobics classes. **FACILITIES:** Limited locker room amenities. **SERVICES & FEES:** One-on-one training session $50; annual membership $850; one class $15; five classes (two month expiration) $65; reservations required for all classes.

EQUINOX FITNESS CLUB
897 Broadway ◆ 780-9300
344 Amsterdam Avenue ◆ 721-4200
Hours: Mon - Thurs: 6 am - 11 pm; Fri: 6 am - 10 pm; Sat - Sun: 8 am - 9 pm.

Once upon a time, Lord & Taylor reigned here with Corinthian columns and vaulted ceilings. Now the columns act as room dividers and are flanked by mirrors and the walls are painted subtle shades of gray, blending high-tech with retro nostalgia. The programs and services offered are extensive and inspiring, addressing every fitness need. **FITNESS EQUIPMENT:** Twenty-five TVs are strung along balconies in viewing distance of the 24 Steppers, 22 Cybex bikes and a combination of 26 Lifestride, Star Track and Quinton treadmills. Downstairs offers complete circuits of Cybex weight-resistant equipment plus a full range of free weights. **CLASSES:** Boxing master Michael Olajide holds court, teaching a boxing circuit daily. Other scheduled classes include jazz, body sculpting, aerobics, 21st-century circuit, Qigong stretch, slide and step. **FACILITIES:** Ground-floor sports boutique, spacious locker room with all amenities, steam room and cafe where visitors are welcome to dine. The uptown club recently expanded to include a Wellness center featuring herbology, reflexology, acupuncture and aromatherapy. **SERVICES & FEES:** One-on-one training session $25; fitness evaluation; nutritional counseling; sports medicine and physical therapy staff available by appointment; Swedish, deep tissue, acupressure, sports and pre-natal massage $60; 30-minute pep-up massage $39; membership $1,108 plus monthly $85; member guest no fee (reservation required); guest fee (general public) $26.

EXCELSIOR ATHLETIC CLUB
301 East 57th Street ◆ 688-5280
Hours: Mon - Fri: 6 am - 10 pm; Sat - Sun: 8 am - 8 pm.

Bustling and congenial, this privately-owned club enjoys a low profile while nurturing a diverse and loyal membership. In the sprawling 19,000 square feet occupying one floor, everything fits comfortably and traffic moves affably. Complimentary breakfast draws an early crowd and pre-lunch hours are abuzz with seniors. The spa program offers an impressive sampling of treatments. The pièce de résistance is the ping-pong table located poolside. Regular tournaments have become quite the thing. **FITNESS EQUIPMENT:** An extensive array of equipment including VersaClimber, treadmills, NordicTrack, LifeCycles, StairMasters and rowing machines. **CLASSES:** Full range of step, low-impact aerobics, body sculpting,

yoga, boxing and water programs. **FACILITIES:** All amenities, locker room attendant, sauna and steam room.
SERVICES & FEES: One-on-one training session $40 -
$70; nutritional counseling; physical therapy; Swedish,
deep tissue, reflexology, energy balancing and sports
massage available by appointment $55; annual member-
ship $950; initiation $300; guest fee $25; International
Health and Racquet Sports Association reciprocity.

EXECUTIVE FITNESS CENTER
at THE NEW YORK VISTA HOTEL
3 World Trade Center ◆ 466-9266
Hours: Mon - Fri: 6 am - 9:30 pm; Sat - Sun: 8 am - 7 pm.

It's back! Looking to recapture its 1,600-plus membership
from pre-explosion days, the Fitness Center has added
new gusto to its facility. Known for professionalism, this
spacious, low-key club has frequently been cited as one
of the top corporate facilities in the country. **FITNESS
EQUIPMENT:** Cybex, Hammer Strength, Universal,
Nautilus, free weights, Lifestride treadmills, LifeFitness
recumbent bikes and StairMaster Cross-Aerobics. The
Tectrix VR Max Bike, Tectrix ClimbMax, and Cybex bikes
are strategically placed to capture panoramic Hudson
views. Overlooking the 50 X 20-foot pool, the upper
balcony houses additional weight-resistance equipment
and doubles as a track. **CLASSES:** Full range of aerobic,
step, circuit, toning and water exercise programs.
FACILITIES: Racquetball courts, complete amenities plus
steam and sauna in locker rooms. **SERVICES & FEES:**

Laundry service, exercise clothing provided; one-on-one training session $40; personal fitness evaluations and exercise prescriptions; in-house nutritionist and physical therapist; Swedish, deep tissue, Shiatsu, acupressure and sports massage by appointment; annual membership $1,399; reciprocity with The Fitness Company.

GOLD'S GYM
1635 Third Avenue ◆ 987-7200
1736 Shore Parkway, Brooklyn ◆ 718-714-4653
Hours: Mon - Fri: 5 am - 12 am; Sat - Sun: 6 am - 11 pm.

If you're looking for a social outlet, go elsewhere. Getting results—losing body fat, toning and building muscles—is Gold's raison d'être. Members receive six free personal training sessions and a 12-week guaranteed nutrition program based on the Apex system. **FITNESS EQUIPMENT:** In this 30,000 square-foot cross-training center, 25,000 square feet is devoted to free weights and weight-resistance equipment including Hammer Strength, Icarian, Panatta Sport, Cybex and LifeCycle. **CLASSES:** Aerobics, toning, Tae Kwon Do, boxing with Mark Breland, pre- and post-natal and aqua aerobics. **FACILITIES:** 50-foot lap pool with spacious deck area (at Third Avenue location only), outdoor restaurant on esplanade adjacent to club, juice bar and snack bar on premises, whirlpool, steam room, sauna, tanning beds and complete amenities in locker rooms. **SERVICES & FEES:** Physical therapy; baby-sitting; one-on-one training session $75; Swedish, deep tissue and Shiatsu massage $40; annual membership

$1,267; guest fee $20. Membership prices lower at Brooklyn location.

MANHATTAN PLAZA HEALTH CLUB
482 West 43rd Street ◆ 563-7001
Hours: Mon - Fri: 6:45 am - 10 pm;
Sat - Sun: 8:30 am - 7 pm.

Since 1982, this 'Country Club' of health clubs has developed a loyal following with its conscientious price tag and aristocratic tastes. Here you can swim in the lap of luxury in a 75-foot pool, lounge in a whirlpool, sunbathe nestled among 16-foot palm trees, book a massage and linger over lunch at the country-style restaurant. Or exercise your options: Play tennis, rock-climb, take a class or use the facilities. **FITNESS EQUIPMENT:** Spacious cardio and weight-training area includes StairMasters, Quinton treadmills, NordicTracks, Gravitron, Concept II rowers, Cybex bikes, Upper-Body Ergometers, Universal, Eagle, Cybex and free weights. **FACILITIES:** 20-foot high rock-climbing wall with over 40 routes, five tennis courts (leagues, tournaments and game-matching organized). **CLASSES:** Stretch, yoga, body sculpting, jazz, Young at Heart, water exercise and aerobics. **SERVICES & FEES:** Spacious locker rooms plus steam room; Swedish and Shiatsu massage; one-on-one training session $20 - $40; annual membership $850; corporate rate $750; rock-climbing wall membership $425; guest fee $15; indoor parking after 5:00 pm weekdays and all day on weekends $2.50.

NEW YORK HEALTH & RACQUET CLUB
39 Whitehall Street ◆ 269-9800
24 East 13th Street ◆ 924-4600
132 East 45th Street ◆ 986-3100
20 East 50th Street ◆ 593-1500
110 West 56th Street ◆ 541-7200
1433 York Avenue ◆ 737-6666
HRC Indoor Golf ◆ 422-Golf
Hours: Mon - Fri: 6 am - 10 pm; Sat: 9 am - 6 pm;
some locations open Sundays.

The New York Health & Racquet Club gained a reputation in fitness in 1972 and has been expanding ever
since. With the introduction of the mega facility in 1987,
the club managed to feature fitness as a way of life,
replete with the social-club trappings of yacht parties,
miniature and simulated golf and an emporium of fitness
options. Workout choices run the gamut with a multitude
of classes and an impressive array of cardio and weight-
training equipment. The other locations offer scaled-
down versions of the Whitehall Street flagship. Social
programming is ambitious and Sunday brunch on the
yacht is still a popular attraction. **FITNESS EQUIPMENT:**
More than 100 pieces of cardiovascular equipment,
including Cybex, Nautilus, StairMaster, Gravitron,
NordicTrack, LifeRowers, LifeCycles, Quinton treadmills,
LifeCircuit and Keiser line plus a full range of free
weights. **FACILITIES:** Restaurant on premises, 1/20 mile
wraparound track, squash, racquetball, basketball, tennis
at various locations, 60-foot swimming pool surrounded
by built-in fish tanks, full locker amenities plus a steam

room and coed whirlpool. **CLASSES:** Full range of aerobic, step, circuit, body sculpting, boxing, water exercise, roller-blading, Tae Kwon Do, T'ai Chi, yoga and scuba diving. **SERVICES & FEES:** Baby-sitting; one-on-one training, 10 sessions $395; Swedish, Shiatsu and sports massage by appointment $55; annual membership $1,175 (specials frequently available); indoor golf and Country Club additional fee; corporate membership $975; member guest $20. All locations offer reciprocity.

PENINSULA SPA
700 Fifth Avenue ◆ 247-2200
Hours: Mon - Fri: 6 am - 9 pm; Sat - Sun: 8:30 am - 7 pm.

Nestled on the top three floors of the hotel, this private utopia is your cocoon. Membership is purposely small, service is the name of the game and you are the star. Perched atop Manhattan's skyline, sprawling sun decks and terraced patios provide dining and lounging options. It's your club and you are always greeted by name. **FITNESS EQUIPMENT:** LifeSteps, LifeCycles, StairMasters, Concept II rowers, NordicTrack, treadmills, LifeRowers, full range of Cybex strength-training equipment, plus free weights. **CLASSES:** Full range of aerobics including aqua aerobics, body sculpting, step, yoga and T'ai Chi. **FACILITIES:** Swimming pool, luxurious locker room with full amenities, eucalyptus steam rooms, sauna, whirlpool. **SERVICES & FEES:** One-on-one training session $60; Swedish, Shiatsu, sports, reflexology, phyto-aromatic and toning massage $40 - $75; body treatments include seaweed wrap, body masque, body waxing and slimming wrap $75 - $100; facials $70 - $85; weekend spa package $175 (available to non-members); clothing provided and serviced; monthly membership $180 plus initiation fee $2,600; guest fee $35; hotel guests complimentary.

PRINTING HOUSE FITNESS AND RACQUET CLUB
421 Hudson Street ◆ 243-7600
Mon - Fri: 6 am - 11 pm; Sat - Sun: 8 am - 8 pm.

This westside club has it all—beautiful views from the fitness center, sprawling outdoor decks with plantings and a small but charming outdoor pool. Spaciously laid out over three floors, there's plenty of room for the 2,400 members to roam and innumerable options to choose from. The transient European clientele adds a certain panache. Try the Kundalini yoga on the rooftop with Ajeet. **FITNESS EQUIPMENT:** Quinton/Trotter treadmills, StairMasters, VersaClimber, Schwinn Airdynes, LifeCycles, Concept II rowers, full range of Cybex, Nautilus and free weights. **CLASSES:** Aerobics, aerobox, body sculpting, yoga, Hip-Hop, step and water exercise. **FACILITIES:** Eight racquetball courts, two international squash courts, three American hardball courts (tournaments, leagues and game-matching organized). Spacious locker rooms, whirlpool, steam and sauna, plus all amenities. **SERVICES & FEES:** Ten massage therapists, nutritionist and sports podiatrist available; one-on-one training session $45; Swedish, deep tissue, medical, sports, Shiatsu, reflexology massage $50; squash and racquetball lessons $30 - $50; annual membership $1,099; racquet membership only $250 plus court time. Classes-only membership $699; guest fee $15/fitness; $10/aerobics and racquet sports.

PROFILE HEALTH SPA
52 East 42nd Street ◆ 697-7177
Hours: Mon - Fri: 6 am - 9 pm;
Sat - Sun: 9:30 am - 5:30 pm.

For women only. Busy female executives are finding the right combination of fitness and relaxation in this spacious, congenial club owned by Joyce Laitman. Even the equipment is designed with women in mind: The weight-resistance equipment is set at five-lb. increments. The single glassed-in studio holds 70 comfortably and the programming is ambitious. **FITNESS EQUIPMENT:** StairMasters, Trotters, LifeCycles, Treadmills, Cybex, Nautilus, full range of free weights and the David line of weight-resistance equipment. **CLASSES:** Aerobics, body sculpting, absolutely abs, step, cardio challenge, aerobox and low-impact. **FACILITIES:** Spacious locker room with full amenities, steam and sauna. A small pro shop sells exercise clothing and refreshments. **SERVICES & FEES:** One-on-one training, one half hour $35; Swedish and Shiatsu massage $70; all services by appointment; annual membership $700 ($59 monthly payment plan); two years $800; guest fee $15 (Mon - Wed); free guest entry with member Thurs - Sun.

REEBOK SPORTS CLUB NEW YORK
160 Columbus Avenue ◆ 362-6800
Hours: Mon - Fri: 5:30 am - 11 pm; Sat - Sun: 7 am - 8 pm.

The Eden of fitness . . . six floors and 140,000 square feet of utopia for the ultimate fitness consumer. This sprawling and airy oasis-cum-fitness-sports-spa-and-wellness center opened its doors in March 1995. Chart your course and tell your friends not to call—you're on vacation! Lounge on the sun deck or meet and greet at one of several restaurants and bars: Sidewalk Cafe, Display Cooking and Dining Bar or Club Bar and Grill. **FITNESS EQUIPMENT:** Pump iron in a spectacular weight-training room featuring Nautilus, Cybex, Flex, Hoist, Body Masters, Hoggan, Keiser, Excalibur, Paramount, Ivanko and more. Build stamina with more than 120 pieces of cardio equipment including TrackMaster treadmills, LifeCycles, Cybex bikes, Tectrix BikeMax, ClimbMax Stepper, StairMasters, Step Mill, StairMaster CrossRobics, NordicTracks, VersaClimbers and Concept II rowing machines. **CLASSES:** Dozens of exercise programs in two 2,500 square-foot studios include Step Reebok, Slide Reebok, Step Reebok Circuit, aerobics, yoga, T'ai Chi, Pilates and body sculpting. **FACILITIES:** Team up with the pros for a game of basketball, volleyball, soccer; join a league— there are two regulation-size full-court gymnasiums with viewing stands; or try the sports simulator featuring golf, skiing, kayaking, wind surfing, boxing and more. The 1/6 mile outdoor running track spans the perimeter and accommodates in-line skating. Climb a 45-foot rock wall ascending three floors, do laps in the 75-foot pool, try one of several water exercise programs or relax in the spacious and well-appointed locker rooms with steam, whirlpool and sauna bath. A full service salon offers mud packs, herbal mineral wraps, seaweed body treatments, salt scrubs, facials, manicures and pedicures. **SERVICES & FEES:** Swedish, Shiatsu, sports and reflexology massage. Reebok has also teamed up with the Sports Training Institute to provide physical therapy, nutritional counseling, one-on-one training and wellness programs addressing smoking cessation, CPR and stress reduction. Did I leave anything out? Oh, bring the kids: Reebok has allocated 4,000 square feet for sports and fitness programs for ages 6 months to 17 years; monthly membership $120 plus initiation fee $1,000 includes free training session and complete fitness evaluation; guest fee $25.

SHERATON MANHATTAN FITNESS CENTER
at the SHERATON MANHATTAN HOTEL
790 Seventh Avenue ◆ 581-3300
Hours: Mon - Fri: 6 am - 9 pm; Sat and Sun: 8 am - 8 pm.

The action at this quiet facility centers around the pool. Aquasize and Hydrotone (plastic water weight) exercise programs are scheduled daily; swim lessons are also available. Most people come to swim laps in the 50 x 20-foot heated pool. The area around the pool is spacious and well maintained with a small exercise room adjacent as well as a sun deck where lunch can be eaten outside, weather permitting.

SHERATON NEW YORK HEALTH CLUB
at the SHERATON NEW YORK HOTEL
811 Seventh Avenue ◆ 841-6714
Hours: Mon - Fri: 6 am - 9 pm; Sat - Sun: 8 am - 8 pm.

This recently renovated and refurbished club is so quiet you can almost call it your own. Attracting a corporate clientele, this compact, service-oriented club provides state-of-the-art cardiovascular and weight-training equipment all in one room, expediting the workout process. TVs and music-channel monitors are accessible from most workout stations. You can definitely do it all in an hour, give or take an extra 15 minutes for a sauna or steam bath. **FITNESS EQUIPMENT:** ClimbMax, LifeCycles, NordicTrack, LifeSteps, full-circuit Cybex weight-resistance equipment, Smith, Paramount and free weights. **FACILITIES:** All amenities in locker rooms. **SERVICES & FEES:** One-on-one training $40; Swedish, Shiatsu, deep tissue, acupressure and sports massage by appointment $50; annual membership $799 (either location); $999 (to use facilities at both locations); hotel guest fee $6/day; outside guests $20/day.

SOHO TRAINING CENTER
110 Greene Street ◆ 219-2018
Hours: Mon - Fri: 6:15 am - 10 pm; Sat: 8 am - 6 pm;
Sun: 9:30 am - 4 pm.

You can train upstairs with twelve staff trainers plus a full circuit of weight-resistance equipment, cardiovascular options and free weights. Or, you can measure your mettle with the pros downstairs in Thai boxing, kick boxing, Tae Kwon Do, T'ai Chi and women's defense classes. If you opt for membership, you can enjoy unlimited usage of both. And, you can stay for actor stunt-training sessions for films featuring martial art scenes. **FITNESS EQUIPMENT:** StairMasters, Concept II rowers, Upper-Body Ergometer, Quinton treadmills, NordicTracks and Tectrix bike, weight-resistance by Nautilus, Keiser and Body Master and Advanced Free Weight system. **FACILITIES:** All amenities available in locker rooms. **SERVICES & FEES:** 45 minute one-on-one training session $40; 15 sessions $525; optional fitness evaluation by staff exercise physiologist $125; massage by appointment $75; annual membership $649; one class $15; 10 classes $95; class cards and one-on-one sessions available to non-members.

UNITED NATIONS PARK HYATT HEALTH CLUB

1 United Nations Plaza ◆ 702-5016
Hours: Mon - Fri: 6:30 am - 10:15 pm;
Sat - Sun: 6:30 am - 10:15 pm.

Fitness discretely and unobtrusively available to hotel guests, the diplomatic community and neighborhood residents. Located on the 27th floor of the Park Hyatt, this private oasis caters to a limited membership of 300 who are privy to spectacular views of the East River and a quiet, elegant ambiance. Programs focus on cardio fitness, weight-training and swimming. One tennis court can be rented hourly by members or guests. **FITNESS EQUIPMENT:** Cybex, LifeCycle, StairMaster, Gravitron and LifeRowers, as well as weight-resistance equipment. **FACILITIES:** Marble-lined locker rooms with showers, sauna, lockers and all amenities. **SERVICES & FEES:** Swedish and Reflexology massage available by appointment $50; guest massage $65; annual membership $1,300; hotel guests complimentary; outside guests $25; tennis court $55 - $65; non-members can book court time.

VERTICAL CLUB
330 East 61st Street ◆ 355-5100
350 West 50th Street ◆ 265-9400
335 Madison Avenue ◆ 983-5320
139 West 32nd Street ◆ 465-1750

They opened their doors in 1978, seeking an elite clientele and offering a megadose of fitness options. It's been a
revolving door ever since. There are 10,000 members,
half of whom joined upon its opening. Imus still goes,
and so does Brooke. The crowd that didn't find a husband
left. There are models, muscle men, workers, celebs,
wannabes and others, all pumping away. What would
happen if another club opened nearby? **FITNESS
EQUIPMENT:** The fitness floor is enormous with members on row after row of top-of-the-line StairMasters,
Cybex bikes, 40 Treadmills, 20 Life Steps, Trotters, five
Gauntlins and Treadwall. Weight-resistance equipment
includes Hammer Strength, Nautilus, Gauntlet, Cybex,
Eagle, Icarian and free weights. Surprisingly, there are no
waiting lines—it's just very busy. **FACILITIES:** 1/10 mile
running track, tennis courts (six indoor, two outdoor),
three racquetball courts and four squash courts, 20 x 40-
foot lap pool with adjacent communal whirlpool,
spacious locker room with attendants, all amenities, plus
steam and sauna, juice bar and concession stand.
CLASSES: 75 wired-for-fitness instructors teach on a rotating basis and classes are offered hourly in the open
amphitheater studio. Aerobics is still the main event, but
others include body sculpting, slide, step, stretch, Tae
Kwon Do, yoga and boxing. **SERVICES & FEES:** One-on-

one trainers available by appointment $45; Swedish, medical, Shiatsu, deep tissue massage $55; racquetball and squash courts $12; racquetball lessons $40; annual membership $1,247; two years including passport privileges $1,559; laundry and locker service $375; annual membership with tennis $3,120; court fees $40; guest fee $25; club reciprocity honored at all 350 Bally clubs nationwide.

WORLD GYM
1926 Broadway ◆ 874-0942
264 Bayridge Avenue, Brooklyn ◆ 718-680-0059
Hours: Open 24 hours Mon - Fri; Sat - Sun: 7 am - 9 pm.

A gym in all its glory. Methodically laid-out work stations with tons of top-of-the-line equipment to work upper and lower body, separate stations for arms and abs, a full range of cardio-fitness options and a free-weight room that's hard to beat, have all wooed building residents and local network executives as members. Staked out on the second floor, this 24,000 square-foot facility overlooks Lincoln Center. Twin aerobic studios provide a roster of classes featuring celebrity teachers. **FITNESS EQUIPMENT:** Hammer Strength, Smith, multiple sets of free weights, full range of Cybex equipment for upper and lower arms, chest and abdominals. Numerous steppers, LifeStep, Quinton and Lifestride treadmills, cross-country ski machines and more. **CLASSES:** More than 120 offered weekly in step, low-impact, yoga, T'ai Chi, meditation, slide, box aerobics and funky dance. **FACILITIES:**

Spacious locker room. **SERVICES & FEES:** Steam and towel service; one-on-one training session $30- $50; Swedish, deep tissue, Shiatsu and sports massage by appointment $50; baby-sitting $3; annual membership $775; senior citizens $550; students $600; corporate rates available; guest fee $17; ten visits $125 (three-month expiration). Reciprocity with more than 300 World Gyms worldwide.

 The Ys

92nd STREET Y CENTER FOR HEALTH, FITNESS & SPORT
1395 Lexington Avenue ◆ 415-5729
Hours: Mon - Thurs: 6 am - 10:30 pm; Fri: 6 am - 8 pm;
Sat: 6 am - 10:30 pm; Sun: 8 am - 8 pm.

Founded over a century ago, this Y's mega-facility boasts 92,000 square feet dedicated to providing fitness programming for everyone. It also enjoys an enviable reputation as a world-renowned cultural arts center, attracting well-known guest speakers and performing artists. With spacious facilities laid out over several floors, programming is ambitious and addresses many aspects of fitness, wellness and organized sports. **FITNESS EQUIPMENT:** Two full Cybex weight-resistance circuits plus free weights. Cardio equipment includes LifeCycles, Life Step, Quinton treadmills, StairMaster, Concept II rowers, Schwinn Airdynes, LifeRowers, VersaClimber, Gravitron, Upper-Body Ergometers and NordicTrack. **CLASSES:** More than 80 adult classes offered weekly in aerobics, yoga, boxercise, step, body sculpting, roller-blading, T'ai Chi, Tae Kwon Do, circuit training, water exercise, pre- and post-natal and Lamaze. Adult swim programs include instruction, competitive swimming, life-guard training and scuba diving. Classes for children include swimming for tots, pre-schoolers and teens, Jam

Aerobics, in-line skating, Fun Aerobics, boxercise, youth boxing, karate, self-defense and gymnastics. **FACILITIES:** 75-foot swimming pool with two adjacent whirlpools, 1/32 mile indoor track, soccer, basketball, volleyball and racquetball courts with games, leagues and tournaments organized regularly. Locker room with full amenities, plus steam, sauna and whirlpool. **SERVICES & FEES:** Baby-sitting; tennis instruction; one-on-one training session $35; racquetball court rental $12; Swedish, Shiatsu, and sports massage by appointment $40 (members); non-members $50; annual membership $625 (off-peak hours); peak hours $992; $95 for one month; guest fee $20; day pass without membership available; reciprocity with more than 125 other centers throughout the U.S. and Canada.

WEST SIDE YMCA
5 West 63rd Street ◆ 787-1301
Hours: Mon - Fri: 6:15 am - 10 pm; Sat: 8 am - 8 pm; Sun: 9 am - 7 pm.

It's about community. Built in 1929, this landmark West Side YMCA defies identity. Both school and hotel, it has managed to catapult itself into the 21st century of fitness. Sprawled over five floors, it unfolds in a maze of rooms, nooks and crannies where programming is ambitious and aims to please every age group. You can spar, join the basketball team, gather for Seido karate, or swim in a luxurious setting enhanced by Renaissance Italian and Spanish tile work. Take a class, pump iron or relax. It's all here and it's friendly, too. **FITNESS EQUIPMENT:** Three studios equipped with 15 Universal and LifeCycles, 12 StairMasters, Body Masters Squat machine, Smith and Cybex weight-resistance pieces, plus Gravitron, Tectrix and a separate, spacious free-weight room. **CLASSES:** For youths, adults and seniors, more than 90 aerobic classes weekly, kick boxing, martial arts, yoga, Feldenkrais, aqua aerobics, step, jazz, circuit and pre-natal. **FACILITIES:** 1/23 mile cantilevered track, four racquetball and two squash courts, two swimming pools: 75 x 25-foot, 60 x 20-foot, steam and sauna in locker rooms with limited amenities and cafeteria. **SERVICES & FEES:** A broad range of wellness programs; organized basketball and volleyball games; squash lessons; one-on-one training session $40; Swedish and Shiatsu massage $50; annual membership $660 with initiation $60; family plan $720 - $1,020; three months membership $225 (no initiation fee); guest fee $15; hotel guests complimentary; reciprocity with other select YMCAs; carte blanche or minimum-fee reciprocity offered at thousands of affiliated Ys worldwide.

CHINATOWN YMCA
100 Hester Street ◆ 219-8393

HARLEM YMCA
180 West 135th Street ◆ 281-4100

McBURNEY YMCA
215 West 23rd Street ◆ 741-9210

VANDERBILT YMCA
224 East 47th Street ◆ 756-9600

All these Ys have individual programming and facilities.
Call specific locations for details.

❀ One-on-One Training

With bulging muscles, a Fabio haircut and a one-word name, usually two syllables at most, the stereotypical personal trainer gets spoofed mercilessly. In fact, being a personal trainer is serious business. A skilled trainer can develop a regimen perfectly tailored to your needs, combining cardiovascular and strength-training work as needed. And with fees that range from $75 upwards for a one-on-one session, the business of finding the right trainer is pretty serious, too.

A good way to select a trainer is to choose someone certified by the American College of Sports Medicine, which has a nationally recognized certification program for trainers. Some trainers are qualified physical therapists or movement analysts as well. Also worth noting is where the trainer works—some are affiliated with gyms and spas, others make "house calls" to the club of your choice. The following are some of the best personal trainer clubs and facilities.

ALINE FITNESS, INC.
230 East 53rd Street ◆ 759-4689
Hours: Mon - Fri: 6 am - 8 pm; Sat: 8 am - 1pm;
closed Sun.

Here is "training for life", a step-by-step approach for developing fitness skills. Under the guidance of owner Elizabeth Trindade, clients are trained in developing correct body posture, the key to obtaining fitness benefits and ensuring a safe workout. All programs are custom tailored for overall conditioning, cardiovascular training, pre- and post-natal, and post-menopause. Trindade will meet you at your place or hers, or take you for a roadie. Her "city circuit" session will find you exploring the city's architecture while getting a cardiovascular workout, practicing lunges on park benches or doing a round of push-ups on scaffolding. Or ask Antonio, her husband and partner, to escort you on a ten-mile run or any workout. Aline's Strollercize program is receiving kudos from post-natal moms. Classes meet in Central Park and start with a power walk; bring stroller and baby! Six additional trainers are on staff. **SERVICES & FEES:** One Strollercize class $15; eight classes $79; at-home training services $65 - $75; 12 sessions $600; massage available by appointment $65 - $100.

B. FIT NETWORK
1 (800) 856-BFIT

Looking for a trainer in Albuquerque? Just because you're going to be out of town doesn't mean you have to be out of shape. The B. Fit Network pairs clients with suitable trainers anywhere in the U.S. and select European cities. There's no charge to register. Trainers are faxed your personal training needs and come equipped with a gym bag full of light equipment. If your hotel has a gym, the trainer will take you through your regular routine there. **FEES:** $75 - $100.

CASA
48 East 73rd Street ◆ 717-1998

Sally and Chris Imbo are taking one-on-one training to new heights. Their private club is meticulously laid-out over two floors of their townhouse. No sweating with the masses, membership has a ceiling of 50 people and no more than three occupy the premises at any given time. Chris is the creator of the Peak 10 workout regime and oversees all the programming. Buying into their regime guarantees you on-going personalized attention by one of the five in-house trainers. **FITNESS EQUIPMENT:** The workout stations include a complete range of cardiovascular and weight-resistance equipment plus free weights. Regular jaunts to the park are also on the menu, where you navigate hills and other challenging terrain as you do squats, lunges and push-ups. **FACILITIES:** Locker rooms are plush and all amenities are supplied. **SERVICES & FEES:** Massage available by appointment; one-on-one session $75 - $125; annual membership $5,000. Call to schedule an appointment.

CENTER FOR OSTEOPATHIC MEDICINE
41 East 42nd Street ◆ 685-8113
Hours: Mon - Thurs: 7 pm - 8 pm; Fri: 7 am - 5 pm;
Sat: 9 am - 3 pm; closed Sun.

Run as an orthopedic and sports medicine facility under the direction of founder Dr. Richard Bachrach, the center focuses on prevention, diagnosis, rehabilitation and treatment of acute and chronic musculoskeletal conditions related to sports injuries. One-on-one treatment sessions are conducted by physical therapists. Rehabilitation is conducted by movement analysts skilled in the Alexander technique, Bartenieff fundamentals and Pilates. Also available is Back Education, a special program designed to provide clients with the necessary tools for long-term back care management, including guidelines for stretching, strengthening and postural exercises. **FITNESS EQUIPMENT:** Trotter treadmill, Precor stepper, Tunturi bikes, MaxiCam free weights and Total Gym, a specially-designed stretching and strengthening machine used primarily for physical therapy. **SERVICES & FEES:** Physical therapy session $110; Shiatsu, sports, medical and connective-tissue therapy massage $55 for one half hour; nutritional counseling $80 for one half hour; acupuncture treatment session $110; all services by appointment only.

DEFINITIONS

139 Fifth Avenue ◆ 780-0300
39 East 78th Street ◆ 628-1200
712 Fifth Avenue ◆ 977-2727
Hours: Mon - Fri: 6 am - 10 pm; Sat: 8 am - 5 pm;
special appointments only Sun.

Partners Joe Barron and Gary Steinhart are among the pioneers of personal training services. Established in 1983, Definitions offers programming that is ambitious and thorough. Their specialty is sports training, but they also offer programs to address overall conditioning as well as obesity and diabetes. An initial fitness evaluation, provided at no additional charge, includes health and exercise history, blood pressure, sub-maximal testing, orthopedic screening, body composition and strength testing. The staff includes ten certified American College of Sports Medicine trainers, exercise physiologists, movement and massage therapists. Barron and Steinhart run a tight ship, service a limited clientele, provide impeccable customer service and pay vigorous attention to training detail. (The Fifth Avenue facility received the coveted National Design award in 1994.) **FITNESS EQUIPMENT:** Full range of Polaris weight-resistance equipment, Olympic free weights, Quinton treadmill, Gauntlet, StairMaster, Concept II rower, LifeCycle and VersaClimber. **FACILITIES:** Individual cabanas finished in buffed aluminum and copper sheeting provide private shower and dressing areas with all amenities. Permanent lockers are available. **SERVICES & FEES:** Clothing is provided and laundered; one-on-one training session

$50 - $65; 12 sessions $720; Shiatsu, sports, and medical massage by appointment $75; five massages $325.

EXUDE, INC.
47 East 68th Street ◆ 737-2870

CEO Edward Jackowski believes "if you have to leave your home for fitness you will not be consistent, thus you will fail." Since 1985, Exude has trained over 12,000 people in the art of training themselves. Hiring the Exude methodology means buying into a fitness concept that is designed to meet your lifestyle, body type, medical and orthopedic needs and fitness acumen. Initial orientation includes informal testing, body-type assessment and program sampling. Next you are matched with a suitable fitness consultant from a staff of 50 for a six-week program. By the end of that time, you have acquired a personal fitness regime based on self-motivation and results. **SERVICES & FEES:** Fitness orientation $65; at-home equipment package (mat, aerobic bar for calisthenics and stretching, curl bar and jump rope) $112; fitness orientation, at-home equipment package plus a Bodyguard 955 stationary bike $500; six-week program (18 sessions plus diet program) $1,296; reciprocity offered at branch organizations in New Jersey, Connecticut, Florida, Los Angeles and Washington DC. Call to schedule an appointment.

GYROTRONIC EXPANSION SYSTEM
219 West 29th Street ◆ 695-0083

By employing a triple-loop pulley system, Romanian Julio Horvath has discovered a method for moving joints in every imaginable way and integrating the entire body into the process. The six pieces of equipment and 92 exercises he designed provide clients with the greatest range of motion possible. The pulley system distributes weight evenly and provides constant resistance while engaging all limbs simultaneously with unparalleled smoothness in execution and landing. The workout is intensely stimulating, bringing blood to the organs and central nervous system as it releases the spine and strengthens the joints and ligaments. **SERVICES & FEES:** Twelve trainers are on hand to supervise workouts; initiation session $35; one-on-one training session $45-$50; supervised session $16. A teacher training program is offered twice yearly.

HOMEBODIES
1841 Broadway, Suite 510B ◆ 586-7160

The program here starts with a review of your medical history and exercise background. Testing is done next to measure your strength and flexibility, finishing with a three-minute step test with a heart-rate monitor. Custom-tailored programs are designed to meet individual goals and needs. A staff of 22 trainers provides a wide range of expertise in movement arts and strength-training regimes. Programs are designed for your home, office or gym.

Workouts include cardiovascular conditioning, strength training and stretching. Clients are encouraged to purchase Heavy Hands. **SERVICES & FEES:** Fitness evaluation $150; one-on-one session $80. Call to schedule an appointment.

JEAN CLAUDE WEST
27 Bleecker Street ◆ 254-9134
Hours: Mon - Fri: 10 am - 6 pm.

In a class by himself, and well respected by his colleagues, West has moved beyond the Pilates concept to redefine what is a neutral pelvis position and its effect on the lumbar spine. He uses a full range of spring-loaded equipment he designed and built himself, based on the principle of the muscle's elastic ability to contract and spring forward. West interweaves Pilates exercises and joint realignment to correct the body's imbalances. (His specialty is imbalances created from disproportionate limb sizes.) Tactile cues help clients learn to achieve efficient movement patterns while maintaining spinal integrity and proper joint rotation. **SERVICES & FEES:** Five in-house trainers available by appointment; one-on-one session $50.

MATERNAL FITNESS, INC.
4 Park Avenue, Suite 18-J ◆ 213-6949
Group classes at Printing House Fitness and Racquet Club
421 Hudson Street
Hours: Mon - Fri: 10 am - 6 pm.

This is a fitness routine to prepare you for the marathon of labor. Childbirth educator, RN and certified trainer Julie Tupler has designed a comprehensive one-on-one program that teaches moms-to-be a precise exercise regime for strengthening the muscles most taxed during birth. The first of the five-session program is devoted to a health and fitness evaluation and nutritional counseling. The next three sessions include a gentle warm-up, stretching and exercises. The final session provides a series of relaxation techniques and includes an upper-body massage. Your back will thank you. **SERVICES & FEES:** Sessions are available at the studio or at home with one of the 25 staff RNs; one session $75; five session program $345.

PLUS ONE FITNESS
One World Financial Center, 200 Liberty Street ◆ 945-2525
106 Crosby Street ◆ 334-1116
Hours: Mon - Fri: 6 am - 9 pm; closed Sat and Sun.
301 Park Avenue (Waldorf Astoria) ◆ 872-4970;
open Sat and Sun: 8 am - 8 pm.

This is the ultimate in personal training. Every protocol for testing and evaluation, fitness recommendation and treatment is overseen by a staff of physical therapists and exercise physiologists. Or you can exercise your fitness options with Plus Training, a sophisticated computerized system that prescribes daily training routines. Program prescriptions are also available to address rehabilitation requirements, hypertension, physical limitations, pre- and post-natal. **FITNESS EQUIPMENT:** Eagle and Cybex weight-resistance equipment, full range of Universal free weights. Cardio includes LifeStep, LifeCycle, Concept II rowers, Upper-Body Ergometer, Quinton treadmills, NordicTrack, ClimbMax stepper, Fitron cycles and the Bike by Cybex. **FACILITIES:** Locker rooms with full amenities. **SERVICES & FEES:** Fitness evaluation by physical therapist and exercise physiologist includes musculoskeletal evaluation, flexibility and strength testing, cardiovascular capacity and evaluation of body composition $285; one-on-one training session $75; 25 sessions $1,700; Plus Training program session $26; 25 sessions $650; nutritional counseling initial evaluation $125; subsequent visits $75; physical therapy $125 initial evaluation; subsequent visits $105; maximal stress testing $350 (clients); $475 (non-clients); Swedish, Shiatsu, sports, medical, and reflexology massage $65; clothing provided and laundered.

SPORTS TRAINING INSTITUTE
239 East 49th Street ♦ 752-7111
Mon - Fri: 5:30 am - 9 pm; Sat: 8:30 am - 4:30 pm;
Sun: 10 am - 3 pm.

Mike O'Shea, Ph.D., pioneered the concept of personal fitness and has set the pace for defining new standards of excellence ever since. This institute, which he founded in 1975, provides physical therapy and one-on-one training with 25 staff trainers. M.D. referral is required for the evaluation, which includes health history, musculoskeletal and body composition, as well as strength, flexibility and abdominal endurance testing. Programs are designed to maintain fitness goals, meet orthopedic and rehabilitation requirements, provide sport-specific training and address the special needs of clients with diabetes, hypertension, asthma, arthritis and pre- and post-natal. **FITNESS EQUIPMENT:** Cybex, Eagle, Nautilus, Smith, Universal and Keiser, full range of free weights, LifeCycle, StairMasters, Concept II rowers, Upper-Body Ergometers, Quinton treadmills, NordicTracks, ClimbMax stepper, Cross Rubric and VersaClimber. **CLASSES:** Stretch, Feldenkrais and the Alexander Technique, yoga, karate and Tae Kwon Do. **SERVICES & FEES:** Fitness evaluation $250; one-on-one training session $52; 20 sessions $988; physical therapist initial evaluation $100; subsequent visits $90. Shiatsu, sports, Swedish massage $65; 10 sessions $585; 15-minute sports massage $22; ten for $195; no membership requirements.

✳ Yoga & Meditation

For yoga devotees, practicing the ancient breathing techniques and classic postures like Downward Facing Dog and the Cobra can induce a sense of mental and physical well-being. Meditation, done properly, brings on a deep state of relaxation and, some say, dramatically increases energy. And learning to stretch through the postures strengthens the mind and body, leaving the brain tranquil and the joints limber, a potent combination indeed. It's not uncommon to leave a yoga class feeling several inches taller (unfortunately, the sensation passes).

As modern practitioners have adapted traditional Hatha yoga postures, a cornucopia of styles has resulted. Given the growing number of yoga studios and practitioners throughout New York City, it is possible to sample all the strains, from *Astanga* and *Iyengar* to urban and power yoga. The following is a sampling of the many and the best in the city.

THE ENERGY CENTER

53 Wyckoff Street, Brooklyn ◆ 718-596-1751
Hours: Mon - Fri: 9:30 am and 6:30 pm; beginner and
family programs Tues, Thurs and Sat: 4 pm.

Housed in a private carriage house, Brooklyn's Hatha
yoga and wellness center has been providing the community with a roster of programming options to explore
body, mind and spirit since 1991. Director Ed Agolia and
co-director Joyce Cossett combine classic Hatha yoga
practices with Iyengar and Kripalu disciplines. **CLASSES:**
In addition to yoga, the Center offers classes, workshops
and retreats. Programs include the study of *pranayama*
(a breathing practice) meditation, rejuvenation, deep
relaxation, *aryuveda*, nutrition and cooking. **SERVICES &
FEES:** Morning classes are two hours, all others are one
and one quarter hours; one class $12; six classes $50.

HARD & SOFT ASTANGA YOGA INSTITUTE

325 East 41st Street, Suite 203 ◆ 661-2895

Beryl Bender Birch, director, and Tom Birch, co-director,
teach the "power yoga" workout popular among runners
and athletes. Participants also enjoy the vigorous form of
yoga known as *Astanga*: a sequential linking of postures
into a flowing form accompanied by deep yogic breathing.

The practice generates abundant heat, ideal for limbering constrained muscles, ligaments and joints. The pair also run the wellness department at the New York Road Runner's Club. In addition to providing classes, the institute offers other services, such as customized nutritional counseling and bio-mechanical analysis to assist in correcting structural imbalances and weaknesses. Yearly retreats are scheduled in Jamaica during January and in East Hampton throughout the summer. **SERVICES & FEES:** 75-minute classes for beginners and intermediates are available at several locations; one class $14; once a week for six weeks $70; twice a week for six weeks $120. Call for class times.

HIMALAYAN INSTITUTE OF NEW YORK
78 Fifth Avenue ♦ 243-5995
568 Columbus Avenue ♦ 787-7552

This non-profit institute was founded in 1971 by Swami Rama with a mission to blend the ancient wisdom of the East with Western science and technologies. It offers a diverse range of classes and programs that embrace the principles of holistic living and self-development. Classes, workshops, seminars, teacher training programs and retreats are scheduled throughout the year in such areas as Hatha yoga, meditation, biofeedback, stress reduction, diet and nutrition, vegetarian cooking and practical psychology for better living. **SERVICES & FEES:** Open meditation class every Thursday evening 6:00 pm -

7:00 pm, no charge; yoga program (once a week for eight weeks) $65, classes are one and a half hours long. Call for schedule.

INTEGRAL YOGA INSTITUTE
227 West 13th Street ◆ 929-0585
22 West 72nd Street ◆ 721-4000

The Integral Yoga Institute offers classic yoga at its best. Classes focus on bringing the physical, mental and emotional facets of being into balance with an in-drawn meditative attitude. The institute conducts regular retreats at its ashram in Virginia. Disciples often become teachers themselves, following completion of a rigorous teacher training program. **CLASSES:** A wide range of courses includes meditation, deep relaxation, yogic practices and vegetarian cooking, as well as programs on health and healing by regular guest lecturers. **FACILITIES:** A comprehensive bookstore and one of the best health supermarkets in the city can be found at the 13th Street location. **CLASSES:** 75-minute yoga classes for beginners, intermediates, pre-natal, seniors and people with HIV, as well as meditation, *kirtan* (cleansing practices), and *satsang* (group meditation, mantra chanting and lecture). **FEES:** One class $9. Call for schedule.

IYENGAR YOGA INSTITUTE OF NEW YORK
27 West 24th Street ◆ 691-YOGA

Iyengar said, "If you look after the root of the tree, the fragrance and flowering will come by itself. If you look after the body, the fragrance of the mind and spirit will come by itself." Iyengar has become one of the most popular forms of yoga practiced today and is taught at schools and centers worldwide. Its goal is the achievement of exact structural alignment which offers both physiological and metaphysical benefits. This is considered "meditation in action" and its integration of core breath work and focused concentration promotes a heightened sense of awareness. **SERVICES & FEES:** 75-minute session $10 - $15 (depending on teacher and class level); no advanced registration required. Call for schedule.

JIVAMUKTI
149 Second Avenue ◆ 353-0214

As Sharon Gannon and David Life explain it, *jiva* means "individual soul" and *mukti* means "liberation." They believe that "stripped of its spiritual essence, yoga becomes nothing more than another vacuous physical exercise." The two offer an invigorating and eclectic class mix combining chanting and meditation with a vigorous form of *vinyasa* (flowing postures). Incense drifts through the spacious double studio. The temperature is a languid 80 degrees. Sixty bodies in flowing motion cast shadows on the purple walls. To the vibrating chant of *OM*—the sound of consciousness, the primal mantra—peace pervades. Classes run one and a half to two hours with all levels welcome. **FEES:** One class $9; special workshops and teacher training programs are scheduled regularly. Call for schedule.

KUNDALINI YOGA with RAVI SINGH
401 Lafayette Street ◆ 475-0212
Hours: Mon - Fri: 9 am and 6 pm; Sat: 9 am, Sun: 3 pm.

In Ravi's words, Kundalini yoga is "a personal trainer, therapist and spiritual adviser all wrapped up into one." It employs powerful breathing techniques in various *asanas* (positions), which draw energy upward, stimulating and purifying the central nervous and glandular systems as this energy passes through each *chakra* (energy center). The ultimate goal is to bring your mind to a state where it can meditate. Breathing exercises are interspersed with periods of meditation and relaxation, during which Ravi proffers ancient words of wisdom for mastering your mind and, in turn, your life. **FEES:** 90-minute class (Sunday classes are 75 minutes) $10.

NEW YORK CENTER FOR KRIPALU YOGA AND HEALTH
890 Broadway, Studio 5-2 ◆ 645-4519

Kripalu yoga takes a Zen approach; it is practiced as a vehicle for entering into a higher state of consciousness.

Each posture is explored in three stages: First, the posture is broken down into micro-movements in order to focus on structural alignment and the conscious internalization of the process. The second stage requires a prolonged holding of the posture during which students follow their own breathing with an unbroken stream of attention. In the third state, the participants surrender to the posture, allowing the inner wisdom of breath (*prana*) to move the body without intervention from the mind. The resulting state is meditation in motion. Classes are held at the New York Center and with teachers citywide. Robyn Ross (212-864-2399) teaches classes regularly in midtown and on the west side. Ketul (212-496-2384) teaches classes daily in his studio on the upper west side. Call the center for additional recommendations. The Kripalu Institute is located in Lenox, Massachusetts, where week-long programs are available by reservation (413-448-3400).

NEW YORK OPEN CENTER
83 Spring Street ◆ 219-2527

The center offers a broad range of classes, workshops, and lectures on fitness, health and philosophy of wellness. Excellent teachers and guest lecturers offer courses in all kinds of body-work and movement methods, including Alexander Technique, yoga, Shiatsu, Pilates, Chen-style T'ai Chi, power yoga, Kripalu and Kundalini yoga. There are programs in various spiritual philosophies and meditation as well as classes in holistic and alternative forms of healing. The center is run as a not-for-profit organization. Costs are minimal and membership is encouraged. Call for a free catalog.

NOLL DANIEL URBAN YOGA WORKOUT
900 Broadway ◆ 505-0902

Colored stage lights cast shadows changing from purple to orange, and rhythmic tempos accompany this accessible type of yoga workout. Noll masterfully choreographs the process of stilling the mind and stimulating the energy centers. Students move from the stillness of prolonged postures to a dynamic, intense state through the continuous flow and repetition of movements. Breathing exercises are interjected to stimulate and balance the energy centers. Strength and stamina are built through core body work, push-ups and abdominal exercises. Other forms of yoga offered include pre- and post-natal, *vinyasa* (flowing postures), and Yogasol (an athletic yoga) taught by Molly Fox. Classes held seven days a week. **FEES:** One class $12; ten classes $85. Call for schedule.

SIVANANDA YOGA VENDANTA CENTER
243 West 24th Street ◆ 255-4560
Hours: Mon - Sat: 9 am - 9 pm; Sun: 7 am - 9 pm;
Satsang daily at 6 am, Wed at 8 pm and Sun at 6 pm.

This non-profit spiritual organization was founded in 1957 to promote individual and world peace through the teaching of yogic philosophy and practices. Today, there are more than 30 Sivananda yoga centers and eight ashrams worldwide. The center also functions as a community, embracing the four yogic paths: *bhakti* (worship), *raja* (meditation and concentration), *jhana* (introspection) and *karma* (selfless service). **CLASSES:** Hatha yoga, meditation, chanting and yogic philosophy for adults (all levels), children (7 - 13) and seniors. Group vegetarian meals are prepared daily and those wishing to join are welcome. The center sponsors teacher training programs and scheduled retreats at its ashram in the Catskills. **SERVICES & FEES:** One class $8; ten classes $50; meals $6.

WORLD YOGA CENTER
265 West 72nd Street ◆ 877-4153

With a warm, caring, subtle approach to teaching yoga and the dynamics of posture, Ann Farbman founded this center in 1972. Certified by the Integral Yoga Institute and a disciplined follower of Iyengar, Farbman alternates with co-director Nina Patella to teach a combination of traditional and Iyengar yoga, concluding sessions with a short meditation and chant. **CLASSES:** One and a half hours in length with Level I for beginners, Level II for slower students who are older, pregnant, overweight or recovering from back strain or injury, and Level III for more advanced postures. Meditation classes and teacher training programs are also offered. **FEES:** One class $12; eight classes $72. Call for schedule.

YOGA AT NOON
189 Atlantic Avenue, Brooklyn ◆ 718-624-2452

Major corporate types are taking a yoga break at noon
with Carole Forman, and the client roster reads like a
who's who among business moguls. Forman brings
warmth and humor to her classes, cajoling employees to
relax and unwind while tuning into body and mind. She
begins with a brief relaxation period followed by gentle
stretching and concludes with a sequence of postures that
coordinate breath with movement. Adaptations of the
program can be made to address specific needs. The 45 -
60 minute classes are designed to accommodate up to 25
participants. **SERVICES & FEES:** Corporate rate $900 for
eight classes, once a week. Call for schedule.

YOGA ZONE
160 East 56th Street ◆ 935-YOGA
135 Fifth Avenue ◆ 647-YOGA

The gossamer white drapes cascade 20 feet to rest on
white-washed floors. Ready and sitting in lotus position,
the class begins with a guided meditation. Radiating a
silent beam of energy, director Alan Finger coaxes his
students into relinquishing their egos and seeking their
true nature from within. "*Adiom-om-tatsa.* Take the light
within you and spread it into each moment of your life."
Each posture is systematically executed, balancing
and counter-balancing each side of the body to open
the energy channels and re-align the spinal column. To

re-energize the body's *tantiem* (center), the Kapalabhati breath—54 pumping exhalations also known as "bellows breath"—concludes the one and a half-hour session. Have a super wonderful day. Classes meet seven days a week. **FEES:** One class $15; ten classes $125. Call for schedule.

◉ Martial Arts

◉ T'ai Chi

Anyone who has ever visited Hong Kong no doubt has indelible memories of seeing locals practice T'ai Chi in the park during the early morning. A centuries-old strain of meditation and movement, T'ai Chi promotes deep relaxation, stimulates internal engery, known as *chi*, and has long been associated with health and healing.

Though you're more likely to see runners than T'ai Chi practitioners in Central Park, for many New Yorkers this ancient martial art is the ultimate blend of physical and mental exercises. The Cheng form, comprised of 37 slow, studied movements, is most commonly taught here. With legs bent slightly and kept low to the ground for balance, the individual concentrates on transfering energy from one side of the body to the other. Though it takes close to four months to master the choreography, once learned it can be practiced in minutes. The following schools offer instruction.

AHN T'AI CHI STUDIO, INC.

83 Spring Street ◆ 226-6664

Hours: Mon - Thurs: 6 pm, 7 pm, 8 pm.

Director Don Ahn was a student of the late Great Grand Master Cheng Man Ch'ing and has been passing the Yang lineage of T'ai Chi down to his students for more than 30 years. Ahn focuses on integrating the mind, breath and body with T'ai Chi's slow, deliberate movements. Concentration is placed on aligning and balancing the body in each movement to develop "rooting power," the ability to remain firmly fixed in the way roots anchor a tree. Once students have learned the movements, the principles of rooting and yielding are taught through the form Push Hands where, in pairs, students attempt to unroot their opponent by using pushing tactics. **CLASSES:** Available in Chi Kung, T'ai Chi Sword, Push Hands and Chi Body Work, plus seminars and workshops. Classes begin every month and meet two times a week. **SERVICES & FEES:** One month $98; four months $294 (it usually takes four months to learn the choreography). T'ai Chi demonstration on the first Thursday of every month at 8 pm $3.

KENNETH VAN SICKLE
178 Fifth Avenue ◆ 255-0049
NEW AGE SPACE
129 6th Avenue, Brooklyn

Another of Cheng Man Ch'ing's former students, Van Sickle has been practicing T'ai Chi since 1967. He offers private instruction and scheduled classes at several locations. Beginner classes introduce the concept of unlocking the joints to let the energy flow freely and teach the choreography and meaning of the shapes of the movements. The second phase concentrates on developing a deeper understanding of the movements, rooting and the transfer of energy. Application of the concepts is then applied to Push Hands and, later, Sword Form (Van Sickle's specialty). **SERVICES & FEES:** Lessons by appointment $40; at home $75; call for class schedule and location.

SCHOOL OF T'AI CHI CHUAN, INC.
5 East 17th Street ◆ 929-1981
Hours: Mon - Thurs: 9 am - 8:30 pm; Fri: 9 am - 2 pm;
Sat classes at 11 am and 12:30 pm.

The school was established in 1976 under the direction of Patrick Watson, a senior student of Cheng Man Ch'ing. The school's priority is to promote health and relaxation, and classes are taught by teams of instructors who follow the Yang-style short form of 37 movements. Once you learn the sequence, you can practice it daily at home in

7 - 10 minutes. Students are encouraged to repeat classes as necessary or to benefit from 10 to 15 minute quick-fix sessions. **FEES:** Ten classes $150; free sample class every Tuesday 6 pm - 7 pm.

T'AI CHI CH'UAN CENTER OF NEW YORK
125 West 43rd Street ◆ 221-6110
Hours: Mon - Fri: 4 pm - 8:30; Sat: 11 am - 2:30 pm.

At this center classes begin with instruction in Yang short form (37 movements), then move to Yang long form (108 movements). Over time the choreography becomes secondary and the movements are fluid. Intermediate classes teach Push Hands; advanced students learn the practical techniques and theory of sparring—how to utilize yielding, sticking and *chi* power in combat situations—along with the principals of Nei Kung, the mastery of cultivating *chi* more naturally via body alignment. Master C.K. Chu, who has been teaching for 21 years, is the author of several books and conducts all classes himself. **CLASSES:** Offered in T'ai Chi, Push Hands, fighting (levels one, two and three) and Nei Kung. **FEES:** One class $18; four classes $60; 16 classes (two months) $180.

T'AI CHI CHUAN OF PARK SLOPE
38 7th Avenue, Brooklyn ◆ 718-622-6676
Hours: Beginners Tues: 7 pm, Sat: 8 am;
Push Hands Tues: 8 pm.

Sy Tepper, a graduate of Master William C.C. Chen's
program, has been teaching since 1986. Classes follow
the 37 basic movements of the Yang short form. Students
who have mastered the choreography are encouraged to
learn breath and movement coordination to maximize the
health and healing benefits of the form. Advanced
students also learn Push Hands and Sword Form.
SERVICES & FEES: Private instruction available; one class
$17.50; eight classes $95.

TAOIST ARTS CENTER
342 East 9th Street ◆ 477-7055

For over 15 years, founder and director Susan Rabinowitz
has studied T'ai Chi and Chi Kung. Chi Kung is a 3,000
year-old practice used to heal illness, release stress and
slow the aging process by developing *chi*. Her T'ai Chi
Chuan classes follow the 16-move Wu-style short form,
a comprehensive health and relaxation form used to
develop internal energy. Classes in Taoist meditation
focus on stilling the mind, balancing the body's energies
and promoting harmony with oneself and nature. Pa Kua
Chang is the rarest of the internal arts; its technique of fast
hand-change movements is taught here to promote relaxation. **SERVICES & FEES:** Free senior-citizen program held

at the Sirovich Senior Center at 331 East 12th Street; one class $15; Chi Kung based and energy-balancing massage $75. Call for schedule.

WILLIAM C.C. CHEN T'AI CHI CHUAN, INC.
725 Avenue of the Americas ◆ 675-2816

A senior disciple of the late Great Grand Master Cheng Man Ch'ing and a teacher of the Yang form since 1952, Master Chen is recognized internationally for his workshops on the body mechanics of T'ai Chi Chuan to be used in the art of self-defense. The school is an excellent choice for students interested in competition. In addition to mastery of the choreography, classes focus on achieving a deeper understanding of the principles of T'ai Chi. Advanced classes are offered in form refinement and applications in the art of self-defense. **CLASSES:** Available in Push Hands, Yang long form, Yang sword form and Free-Style San-Shou. **FEES:** One class $20; eight classes $124. Call for schedule.

◎ Karate

Like the other martial arts, karate is more than a mere fighting skill; it seeks to unite mind, body and spirit. While essentially a discipline, the martial arts endeavor to make an individual's instincts work to the fullest so he or she is protected at all times. At the center of arts like karate is the Japanese concept of *suki*, which means an unguarded point. People with a lot of *suki* can be vulnerable to accidents and often, by their demeanor, even invite attack. Martial arts seek to purge all *suki* from body and soul.

Karate, built on lightening-quick hand movements and kicking techniques, has passed through many Asian cultures, but the methods seen most frequently in the United States hail from China, Japan and Korea. Styles, training techniques and philosophies vary from school to school, and New York, not surprisingly, has a variety of schools. Here is a sampling of the more popular practices.

CHINESE HAWAIIAN KENPO ACADEMY

360 Seventh Avenue ◆ 564-6542

1487 First Avenue ◆ 744-0795

Hours: Mon - Fri: 10 am -10 pm.

Looking for a training routine without joining the military? Retired marine Jack Shamburger, 5th-degree black belt, believes that "the mind is a weapon, the body is a tool." Kenpo is an eclectic form of karate with roots in Chinese, Japanese and Hawaiian cultures. It's regarded as one of the fastest hand systems, employing the arm, hand and fingers in varying combinations of movements, including twisting, slicing and finger jabbing. The clock method of rotating the body simultaneously with each defense maneuver is used to teach timing, positioning and accuracy. The whole body is utilized, with a focus on spontaneous reaction and fast, fluid motions. Each form encompasses more than 40 movements and each belt level covers two or three forms. Shamburger teaches all classes himself and each session is one and a half hours. **SERVICES & FEES:** The monthly fee of $169 includes unlimited group sessions and two private lessons; an additional $50 is charged as a one-time registration fee for all programs; private lessons $85.

JAPAN KARATE ASSOCIATION OF NEW YORK
2121 Broadway ◆ 799-5500
Hours: Mon - Fri: 6 pm - 8:30 pm; Sat: 10 am.

Sensei Mori, director and 8th *Dan*, runs a *dojo* earmarked by discipline and structure. The orthodox-style *Shodokan* form is taught here, emphasizing the development of professional character and respect towards others. The style embraces a stance that is wide, low and stable with all movement initiated through the hips. The technique uses combinations of fast and slow movements as well as striking and blocking movements, which are predominantly linear. **CLASSES:** A beginner's program is offered each month and covers the basics of stance, posture, coordinated body movement, introduction to the *katas* (forms) and choreographed non-contact fighting. Upon completion, beginners may join intermediate or combination classes. More advanced students practice free sparring to develop timing and strategy for spontaneous response. **FEES:** Three months $245; students 18 and under $215.

RICHARD CHUN TAE KWON DO CENTER
220 East 86th Street ◆ 772-3700
Hours: Mon, Wed, Fri: 4 pm - 7 pm; Tues, Thurs: 12 pm - 8 pm; Sat 11 am - 1 pm.

Chun has been teaching Tae Kwon Do (the Korean form of karate) for sport and competition for more than 33 years. A 9th-degree black belt, he is currently president of the U.S. Tae Kwon Do Association. His staff of 20 handles the children and teen programs. Chun focuses on advanced special training and teacher training, in addition to teaching the women's program. Drilling in the forms to perfect speed and precision of movements is done solo and in pairs following a half hour of calisthenics (knuckle-style and flat-handed push-ups, squats, cardio tune-up). Basic linear kicks plus an elaborate kicking style that encompasses spinning, flying, jumping and turning are practiced. Several students practice contact sparring in preparation for national sports and Olympic competitions. Special training classes are scheduled on Saturdays. **FEES:** 3-month program $120.

S. HENRY CHO'S KARATE INSTITUTE, INC.
46 West 56th Street ◆ 245-4499
Hours: Mon - Fri: 12 pm - 9 pm; Sat: 11 am - 4 pm.

A 9th-degree black belt who was inducted into the Black Belt Hall of Fame in 1971, director and chief instructor Cho started teaching Tae Kwon Do ten years earlier. With two studios and 30 trained teachers on staff, his school teaches basic form, sparring and self-defense. Form classes emphasize strength training and drilling while non-contact sparring classes focus on fighting technique. Students are paired in alternate defensive and offensive positions. Classes are offered at all levels, starting with children five years old. **FACILITIES:** Gym with cardio and weight-training equipment as well as a heavy bag. **FEES:** Three months, once a week $197; three months, six times a week $357.

WORLD OYAMA KARATE
350 Avenue of the Americas ◆ 477-2888
Hours: Mon - Thurs: 7 am - 8 pm; Fri: 6 am - 7 pm;
Sat: 11 am - 1:30 pm; Sun: 2:30 pm - 3:30 pm.

Is it fun to fight? Yes, particularly under the direction of Grand Master Soshu, 9th-degree black belt. The Oyama style practiced here employs several variations of the basic *katas*, addressing self-defense tactics, fighting and general sport. Classes in the spacious studio encompass a stretching routine, training of basic and combination forms, practice sessions with partners and a final ten minutes of full-contact sparring. Shin guards and knuckle-punch shields are required. The school is applications-oriented, producing many black belts and encouraging students to compete in arranged tournaments. Classes are also available for children. **FEES:** Three months of unlimited classes $199; thereafter $49 a month with one class weekly.

WORLD SEIDO KARATE ORGANIZATION
61 West 23rd Street ◆ 924-0511

OLIVER SEIDO KARATE
2628 Broadway ◆ 678-7015

Under the direction of Grand Master Kaicho Tadashi Nakamura, 9th-degree black belt, traditional Japanese karate is practiced here, with the goal of "developing *bushido* spirit, a non-quitting kind of self-discipline that can be applied to every aspect of one's life." The form is very versatile and encompasses a broad range of movements suitable for any level of fitness. Classes begin with a vigorous calisthenic routine, followed by practice of the basic kicks, punches and blocking techniques. The second half of the class focuses on developing fighting strategies for self-defense. Students are paired off and alternate taking offensive and defensive positions. Beginners learn the basic *katas* (forms) of 15-20 movements, while advanced *katas* can include up to 100 movements. Senior students are taught *katas* with weapons as well as light and non-contact sparring. Meditation is part of the training and concludes each session. The *dojo* has two training studios and a separate weight-training facility. Inter-*dojo* and tournaments are scheduled frequently. Qualified teachers are available to provide group instruction for blind, deaf and physically challenged adults and children. **FEES:** $95 a month for unlimited classes. Call for schedule.

WORLD TAE KWON DO ASSOCIATION
47 West 14th Street ◆ 675-8143
Hours: Mon, Tues, Thurs, Fri: 6 pm - 8 pm.

Grand Master Duk Sung Son has been teaching in New York since 1963 and his program reflects one of the five original forms of Tae Kwon Do taught in Korea. Known primarily as a kicking art, the style focuses on integrating front, side and roundhouse kicks with punching and striking techniques. Emphasis is placed on vigorous drilling in the 15 basic combinations of kicking and punching routines. Free-style, non-contact fighting rounds are practiced in groups of three, alternating partners every few minutes to build intuitive anticipation of attack and encourage speed. Everything takes place under the watchful eye of the Grand Master who teaches all classes himself. Taking at least two classes weekly is encouraged. **FEES:** $90 a month.

◎ Aikido

Like yoga, the martial arts tend to be rooted deep in the past. But aikido dates more modestly from 1942, when it was developed by Morihei Ueshiba, a Japanese martial arts expert. Aikido, considered an art as opposed to a fighting art, flourished in Japan during the postwar period, when American occupational forces outlawed the fighting variety of martial arts, like jujitsu. And it is flourishing in New York City today at a variety of *dojos* with soothing surroundings and heavy canvas floor mats.

Aikido, which means "the way to meet the spirit," is based on the concept of natural rhythm: flowing and yielding. It emphasizes being in tune with your opponent so as to sense his intentions and use his own force to defeat him. Physically, this is accomplished through throwing and grappling, but there is, naturally, plenty of mental throwing and grappling as well. In aikido, after all, the mind is trained to lead the body.

AIKIDO GREENWICH VILLAGE
14-16 Waverly Place ◆ 505-6092

This school is affiliated with the Aikido Foundation in Japan. Beginners learn basic footwork, perfect introductory forms and practice *uekemi*—taking the fall. Partners alternate frequently, allowing students to adapt to and harmonize with different types of energy. Advanced students practice breathing exercises and a technique called "unbendable arm" to cultivate *ki*—a power based on the Zen principle that all mental strength comes from one's center. **CLASSES:** Special classes are scheduled for training with weapons; classes for children 6 years and up are also available. **FEES:** $85 a month for unlimited classes. Call for schedule.

NEW YORK AIKIKAI
142 West 18th Street ◆ 242-6246
Hours: Mon, Wed, Fri: 6:45 am - 7:30 pm; Tues and Thurs: 6:45 am - 6:30 pm; Sat and Sun: 11 am - 1:15 pm.

Yoshimitsu Yamada—8th *Dan* is a member of the Superior Council of the International Aikido Federation, author of *The New Aikido Complete* and this school's chief instructor. The school is run as a non-profit membership club whose sole purpose is to provide instruction. Senior students conduct many of the classes. **SERVICES & FEES:** Adult monthly membership with unlimited attendance $120; teens (12 - 18) $60; children (6 - 12) $30.

SHIN BUDO KAI
416 West 14th Street ◆ 691-1378
Hours: Mon - Fri: 5:30 pm - 8:10 pm; Sat: 10 am - 12:10 pm; closed Sun.

Under the watchful eye of school director and *sensei* (master teacher) Shihan Imaizumi, students practice aikido in pairs, changing partners often to improve their adaptive abilities. Key to the movements are footwork, arm positions and throwing techniques. The school teaches a softer landing style than at other aikido studios and training focuses on a wide range of landings to promote suppleness in the joints, flexibility and increased stamina. Advanced students learn forms with weapons, including the *bokken* (wooden sword). **CLASSES:** *Ki* training, basic form and intermediate level. **FEES:** $100 a month for unlimited classes.

✳ Movement & Bodywork

✳ Alexander Technique

The Alexander Technique and Pilates exercise programs are teaching clients basic principles for exercising correctly and more efficiently. Programs focus on mastering body alignment, building a strong center and torso and learning to breathe more efficiently.

Born in 1869, F.M. Alexander was an actor who suffered from chronic hoarseness only when performing. Through self-observation and subtle changes to his postural habits, Alexander was able to cure himself. The basic tenets of what is called the Alexander Technique are based on the dynamic relationship between the head and the spine, which governs the entire body. Alexander termed the relationship the primary control center. Imbalances in this relationship are one of the contributing causes to lower back pain, slipped discs and discomfort in the hips, knees, and other primary joints.

Sessions in the Alexander Technique address learning to release pressure in the musculature and skeletal structure, by bringing awareness to the primary control center. Clients learn to re-define this relationship in walking, sitting and other movements. The goal is to alleviate tensions caused by compression and fixed postural positions. The process is popular among performing artists and those seeking relief from chronic stiffness often induced by poor postural habits.

AMERICAN CENTER FOR THE ALEXANDER TECHNIQUE
129 West 67th Street ◆ 799-0468

Founded in 1964, the center conducts teacher training programs approved by The North American Society of Teachers for the Alexander Technique and provides teacher recommendations.

THE INSTITUTE FOR RESEARCH, DEVELOPMENT & EDUCATION OF THE ALEXANDER TECHNIQUE
74 MacDougal Street ◆ 473-3247

This institute provides individual training sessions as well as on-going training programs for certification. The 1,600-hour course takes over three years to complete. Practitioners are encouraged to hone their skills continually through workshops, apprenticeships and lectures. Three in-house practitioners are available by appointment for one-on-one sessions. **FEES:** Introductory session $60; on-going sessions $30 for 30 minutes; $60 for 45 minutes.

JESSICA WOLF
117 West 13th Street ◆ 691-3941

Directing people through the process of experiencing their bodies has gained Jessica a formidable reputation as a teacher. By observing and identifying daily habits of misuse that create stress and strain, clients learn to discern the continuity of the head and the spine, how to create more space along it where needed, develop more efficient habits and re-map the mind and body to respond accordingly. Beginning with chair work, you discover how the body is organized in preparation for movement. Table work explores the lengthening process. During the sessions, Wolf introduces concepts for using the breath more efficiently, something she developed through her work with respiratory specialist Carl Strough M.D. **FEES:** One session $65.

NEW YORK CENTER FOR THE ALEXANDER TECHNIQUE
245 West 14th Street ◆ 727-0687

This center is run by four certified trainers schooled under the direction of Thomas Lemens, who is well known for his rigorous four-year certification program. One-on-one sessions, which begin with chair work and progress to walking and table work, guide students through the process of understanding the optimum relationship between the head and spine when sitting, walking and standing. Tension-holding patterns are identified and addressed, while verbal cueing and gentle hands-on techniques aid in movement changes. Bringing awareness to the head and spine relationship, lengthening the spinal column and freeing the musculature create a feeling of bodily ease and well-being. **FEES:** $35 - $40 for a half hour session.

✳ Pilates

"Within 10 sessions you'll feel different, with 20 sessions your friends will notice and within 30 sessions you'll have a different body," said Joseph Pilates.

Created in the Twenties, this method has been the exercise of choice among dancers and athletes ever since. Today, Pilates schools are scattered throughout the U.S. and the technique is gaining a reputation for providing state-of-the-art fitness by defying gravity through strengthening and lengthening the spine. All exercises are performed on a spring-loaded apparatus. The mat work is done without equipment and provides an inexpensive way of sampling the basic principles and benefits.

CORFITNESS, INC.
189 Second Avenue ◆ 598-9616
Hours: Mon - Fri: 7 am - 9 pm; Sat: 9:30 am - 6 pm; Sun: 9:30 am - 3 pm.

Well versed in the movement arts of dance and yoga and a student of first-generation Pilates teachers, Cori Doetzer runs a comprehensive studio, with programs addressing overall fitness, sports specific training and rehabilitation. **FITNESS EQUIPMENT:** Her studio boasts a complete range of Pilates equipment including the Wunda Chair, Cadillac, Universal Reformer, Ped-A-Pull, Standing Barrel and Half Barrel. **CLASSES:** A competent staff of four certified trainers teach Pilates Mat classes daily and provide group introduction to Pilates exercise concepts. Educating clients to understand where the breath stops physiologically trains them to guide the breath more fully through a complete range of movement. One-on-one sessions also address specific breathing techniques. **SERVICES & FEES:** Swedish, Shiatsu, deep tissue, medical and sports massage $65; one private session $60; five sessions $250; one semi-private session $30; 10 sessions $250; mat class $10.

DRAGO'S GYMNASIUM
50 West 57th Street ◆ 757-0724
Hours: Mon - Fri: 7 am - 8 pm; Sat 8 am - 2 pm.

For over 52 years, Romana Kryzanowska has been teaching the Pilates method here. Trained by Pilates himself, Kryzanowska has retained the integrity of the original 500-exercise system, passing its legacy on to her many students and future teachers. Beginners will normally cover up to 30 exercises; advanced students up to 100. Building strength through the art of control improves posture, body alignment and relieves back pain. Frequently used for athletic rehabilitation, the slow, controlled movements are ideal for stretching and lengthening ligaments without stressing the joints. Recognized for its unsurpassed benefits, this strength-training program has attracted dancers, gymnasts, athletes and enlightened consumers for years. **FEES:** One session $35; class cards available.

PERFORMING ARTS PHYSICAL THERAPY
2121 Broadway, Suite 201 ◆ 769-1423
Hours: Mon - Fri: 7 am, 12 pm, 6 pm.

Since 1984, Sean Gallagher has been training dancers and fitness enthusiasts in the Pilates method. Several years ago he purchased the Pilates trademark and the right to use the Pilates name. He hired Romana Kryzanowska (see Drago's Gymnasium) to run the teacher training program that is required for certification. **SERVICES & FEES:** Fifteen instructors are on hand to provide one-on-one instruction, or, for the experienced, in duets; one-on-one session $36; class cards available at discounted prices; mat class $10. For a certified instructor in your area contact the New York center, or the Institute of Pilates, Santa Fe, New Mexico: (505) 988-1990.

PILATES PLUS
at PARK AVENUE SOUTH PHYSICAL THERAPY
257 Park Avenue South ◆ 677-7778

When director Luanne Sforza realized that educating rehabilitation clients in Pilates' controlled movements helped stabilize and prevent exacerbation of injuries, she opened her program to include the general public.

FITNESS EQUIPMENT: Cadillac, Reformer, Wunda Chair and Half-Barrel for Pilates as well as cardiovascular and weight-training including NordicTrack, Quinton treadmill, StairMaster, VersaClimber, Concept II rower, Windracer bike, Body Masters, Cybex, Fitron, Upper-Body Ergometers and free weights. **FACILITIES:** Locker room available. **SERVICES & FEES:** Towel service provided; complimentary ten-minute physical therapy consultation available to all clients; one-on-one sessions, duets, and group classes available by appointment; duet sessions $25; Pilates Mat class $15.

ULTIMATE BODY CONTROL
810 Lexington Avenue, Suite 3F ◆ 319-6194
Hours: Mon - Fri: 7 am - 8 pm; Sat: 9 am - 4 pm.

This compact and intimate place is run by a congenial staff with six of Romana's most proficient Pilates trainers available to take you through a challenging private or semi-private workout. Each individually tailored workout is a controlled series of rhythmic movements done on spring-loaded apparatus. The exercises focus on strengthening and stretching through abdominal control and focused breathing. Clients maintain a horizontal position to assure correct spinal alignment and to eliminate stress on the lower back and neck while they focus on mind-body coordination. **SERVICES & FEES:** Sessions by appointment only; private session $60; five sessions $275; semi-private session $30; ten sessions $270.

❀ Neighborhood Index

SOHO/TRIBECA/DOWNTOWN

Ahn T'ai Chi Studio, Inc., pg. 72
Cardio Fitness Centers, pg. 22
Chinatown YMCA, pg. 45
Executive Fitness Center, pg. 27
Jean Claude West, pg. 54
New York Health & Racquet Club, pg. 30
New York Open Center, pg. 65
Plus One Fitness, pg. 55
Soho Training Center, pg. 37

EAST VILLAGE

CorFitness, Inc., pg. 91
Crunch Fitness, pg. 24
Institute for Research, Development & Education
    of the Alexander Technique, pg. 88
Jivamukti, pg. 63
Kundalini Yoga with Ravi Singh, pg. 64
Taoist Arts Center, pg. 75

EAST MIDTOWN

UPPER WEST SIDE

BROOKLYN

MISCELLANEOUS

❀ Subject Index

BABY-SITTING

Aline Fitness, pg. 48
Gold's Gym, pg. 28
Jeff Martin Studios, pg. 5
New York Health & Racquet Club, pg. 30
92nd Street Y Center for Health, Fitness & Sport, pg. 42

BOXING

American Fitness Center, pg. 16
Better Bodies, pg. 19
Club La Raquette, pg. 23
Crunch Fitness, pg. 24
Equinox Fitness Center, pg. 25
Gleason's Gym, pg. 4
Gold's Gym, pg. 28
New York Health & Racquet Club, pg. 30
Soho Training Center, pg. 37

GYMNASTIC PROGRAMS

POOLS & SWIM PROGRAMS

RACQUET SPORTS - RACQUETBALL, TENNIS & SQUASH

ROCK CLIMBING

ROLLERBLADING

RUNNING - INDOOR/OUTDOOR TRACKS

SCUBA DIVING

TEAM SPORTS - BASKETBALL, SOCCER & VOLLEYBALL

About the Author

Fitness enthusiast Kathy Jones is an avid tennis player, biker and hiker. Her workout regime includes weight-training and cardiovascular conditioning mixed with yoga and an occasional Pilates class. For the past two years, she has devoted her time to researching fitness options in New York City. She has conducted over 150 interviews with fitness practitioners and participated in every program she lists.